PORTKEY GAMES

HOGWARTS
LEGACY

THE OFFICIAL GAME GUIDE

PORTKEY GAMES

HOGWARTS
LEGACY

THE OFFICIAL GAME GUIDE

—⊗— *by* —⊗—

Paul Davies and **Kate Lewis**

WARNER BROS.
GAMES

AVALANCHE

WIZARDING
WORLD

PORTKEY
GAMES

Scholastic Inc.

Contents

Introduction

In *Hogwarts Legacy*, an enchanted world is yours to explore as a new student attending the famous school of witchcraft and wizardry. Unlike your peers, you start out under enigmatic circumstances as a fifth-year. There is much to learn, but your thirst for knowledge is huge. Your professors at late-1800s Hogwarts are only too happy to oblige.

Guided by Professor Fig, this journey from new student to legendary graduate is swiftly underway.

Assignments are set, spells and charms acquired, and soon your adventures take you out of the school grounds into the hamlets and wilderness beyond.

After you are sorted in the Sorting Ceremony, class friends eagerly introduce themselves. You will get to know several of your classmates meaningfully, sharing in their ambitions and helping them resolve problems. This being Hogwarts and involving wizardkind, such quests are invariably rich with surprises.

Meanwhile, a plot hatches between two nefarious and extremely powerful enemy factions. Dark witches and wizards led by Victor Rookwood and a goblin rebellion led by the dangerous Ranrok pose a threat that only you can stop.

Both have their sights set on ancient magic. This primal force flows effortlessly through you. Its secrets are known only to a group of hallowed Hogwarts professors collectively known as the Keepers. Although they suspect you are the one to guard the wizarding world against ruthless forces of evil, they must be sure.

To convince them, you will face a series of trials that are as spellbinding as they are terrifying. To succeed, take courage and have your wits about you. Trust your instincts, study seriously, train with reverence, and be bold. Master your rare ability to see traces of, and possibly wield, ancient magic and save the wizarding world.

PART 1:
SETTING
THE STAGE

Your Hogwarts Persona

Before starting your adventure, spend some time choosing how you'll look in the game. You get to decide your gender, face shape, skin tone, and hairstyle. You can even wear a distinctive battle scar.

Your avatar's physical traits cannot be changed once decided. However, new hairstyle, hair color, and makeup options are available at Madam Snelling's Tress Emporium in Hogsmeade. Rare (or higher) items of clothing and accessories have performance benefits, and an enchanted loom can be used to weave gear traits into the clothing that boost attack capabilities and defensive powers.

AVATAR TIP
If you wish to see yourself in this adventure, your avatar may closely resemble your real-life appearance. Or, let the game choose how you look.

Quite the Entrance

An invitation to attend Hogwarts School of Witchcraft and Wizardry is too good to miss. It is highly unusual that you should enroll as a fifth-year, but the professors and students will do all they can to get you up to speed quickly.

Your first test takes place above the clouds. Inside an (apparently) horseless carriage, Professor Fig and Ministry of Magic employee George Osric discuss the rising threat of the goblin rebellion. You take note of the name Ranrok and the object of this goblin's desire: an ornate silver container.

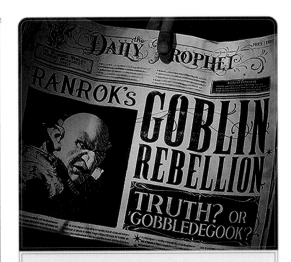

REBELLION BREWING
Ranrok is said to be stoking rebellion in the wizarding world, urging goblins to rise up against wizardkind in shocking acts of violence.

WHAT'S A PORTKEY?

A Portkey is a means of magical transportation. It can be any enchanted object that, once touched, transports the user to a specific location.

Being observant is a necessary skill to navigate the adventures ahead. You must find the answers to progress, but clues are available should you need them. When the carriage is attacked by a dragon and you see a strange glow around the **PORTKEY** container, you and Professor Fig discover you are able to see traces of **ANCIENT MAGIC**. This is an extremely rare talent and one that Professor Fig is keen to investigate with you. Fig will become your mentor and key companion on the many adventures to come.

After the Portkey transports you and Professor Fig to a cave, you get your first taste of exploration. This is where you learn the basic movements— running, jumping, and climbing over rugged terrain.

Fig advises you to drink some **WIGGENWELD POTION** to heal yourself from any injuries sustained during the dragon attack and Portkey travel. When it comes to causing damage of your own, the first target is a magical barrier that is easily shattered with the **BASIC CAST**.

PROFESSOR ELEAZAR FIG

Magical Theory Professor at Hogwarts

Eleazar Fig left behind his aspirations of working for the Ministry of Magic in order to follow his wife, Miriam, around the world as she researched the seeming disappearance of ancient magic. Fig eventually grew weary of this quest and left her to continue on her own while he took on the job of Magical Theory professor at Hogwarts. When Miriam was killed during her travels, Fig felt responsible because he was not there, a guilt that haunts him to this day. He is determined to understand why and how she died and to finish her work. Fig is a kind, knowledgeable professor and will be one of your greatest allies at Hogwarts.

Once through the barrier of what appears to be crystallized stone, you and Professor Fig find yourselves in Gringotts Wizarding Bank.

A banker goblin, perched behind his desk, requires a key to allow you to progress farther into the bank. Luckily this happens to be the Portkey, already in Fig's possession, which opens Vault 12. Elsewhere in your quest such artifacts are well hidden, involve puzzles, and are often guarded by magical beasts!

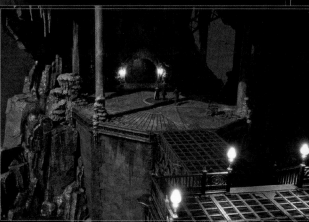

Once you acquire an artifact, however, rewards for progress can be breathtaking. Rushing into the depths of Gringotts, through the cascading Thief's Downfall waterfall, is one such moment.

Professor Fig teaches the spell **REVELIO**, an essential spell that reveals hidden objects and pathways. In the vaults of Gringotts, it reveals an escape route. Once cast, *Revelio* highlights a door with a glowing symbol, similar to that first seen on the Portkey container, indicating the presence of ancient magic.

RANROK

Leader of the Goblin Rebellion

Clever, cunning, vicious, violent, and opportunistic, Ranrok is a goblin overlord and not to be trifled with. He is working with Victor Rookwood to amass the power he believes will help him rebel against wizardkind. He has influenced goblins known as Loyalists to join him in a bid to overthrow wizards, but not all goblins follow his banner, and some actively work against him. He does not hide his disdain for wizardkind and will go to extremes to get the power he wants.

Once through the door, your new surroundings are enveloped by darkness. While moving cautiously between colonnades, Professor Fig teaches you how to use **LUMOS** to light the way. A peculiar flow of energy leads to a concentrated swirl of ancient magic, bringing the reflections of Pensieve Protectors into view . . . though Fig is unable to see them.

Casting *Lumos* allows you to carefully align the reflections of the Protectors, which awakens them. Unfortunately, the armored statues are trained to defend their territory, and without too much warning, you are thrown into combat. You quickly learn the basics. **PROTEGO** conjures a protective shield, and **STUPEFY** stuns your enemies. Once the Protectors are vanquished, you have to witness a Pensieve memory and escape a dramatic encounter with Ranrok before reaching Hogwarts to begin your studies.

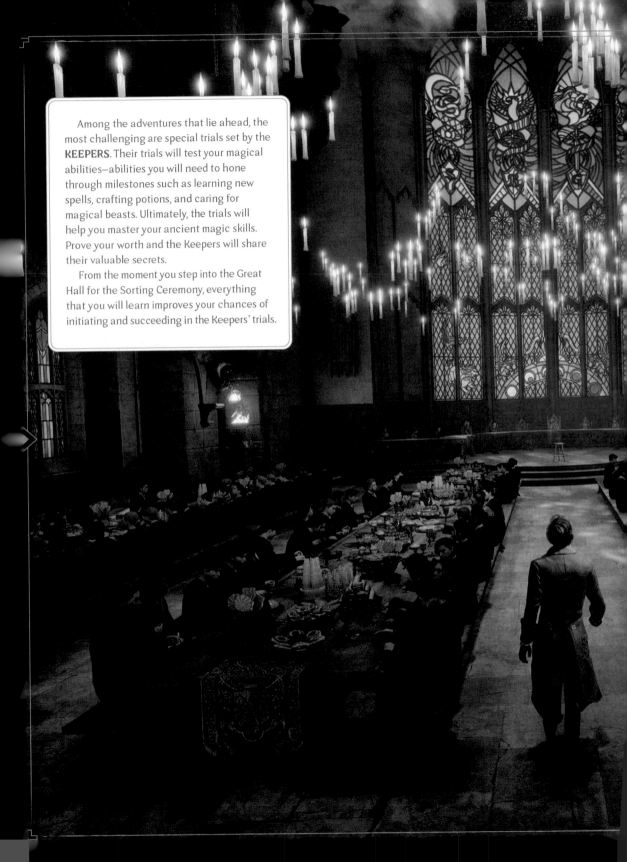

Among the adventures that lie ahead, the most challenging are special trials set by the **KEEPERS**. Their trials will test your magical abilities—abilities you will need to hone through milestones such as learning new spells, crafting potions, and caring for magical beasts. Ultimately, the trials will help you master your ancient magic skills. Prove your worth and the Keepers will share their valuable secrets.

From the moment you step into the Great Hall for the Sorting Ceremony, everything that you will learn improves your chances of initiating and succeeding in the Keepers' trials.

DRESS TO IMPRESS

You arrive at Hogwarts in your travel attire, dusty from battle. Professor Fig casts a quick spell to make you look like a real Hogwarts student.

PROFESSOR MATILDA WEASLEY

Deputy Headmistress and Transfiguration Professor at Hogwarts

Matilda Weasley worked for the Ministry of Magic after she graduated from Hogwarts. She rose through the ranks, her calm presence and extraordinary wandwork making her an invaluable asset. Eventually, while on an assignment for the Ministry, she met Paul— a brilliant, free-spirited wizard working as a curse-breaker. Weasley agreed to leave the stuffy world of bureaucracy and head out to travel the globe with Paul as freelance curse-breakers. Upon returning to teach at Hogwarts, Professor Weasley has found fulfillment in nurturing her students.

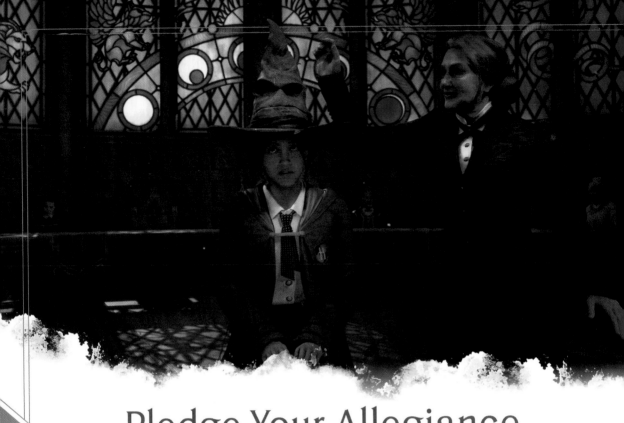

Pledge Your Allegiance

The Sorting Ceremony is a moment to savor, choosing which Hogwarts house best suits your nature. By doing so, you also determine your common room, where you get to know some of your fellow students. Their questioning minds and curious pursuits bring Hogwarts to life in later quests.

In Gryffindor, you'll meet Garreth Weasley, Natsai Onai, Nellie Oggspire, and Cressida Blume. In Hufflepuff, Lenora Abbott, Arthur Plummly, and Adelaide Oakes. Ravenclaw leads you to Amit Thakkar, Everett Clopton, and Samantha Dale. Slytherin points to exploits with Ominis Gaunt, Sebastian Sallow, and Imelda Reyes.

Whichever you choose, the common room and houses are lavishly laid out, making you feel right at home. Not that you'll spend too much time there. You are more likely to be wandering the Forbidden Forest, or some far-flung Dark wizard's encampment!

GARRETH WEASLEY

Fifth-Year Student, Gryffindor

An easygoing, popular boy, Garreth
Weasley is a talented student. However,
he rarely devotes much time to his
schoolwork, instead choosing to
experiment with his own brews of
magical drinks or relaxing on the school
grounds with his friends. He loves his
aunt Matilda, Deputy Headmistress, but
is tired of being under her watchful eye.
He just may ask for your help in
procuring hard-to-find ingredients for
his creative concoctions.

ADELAIDE OAKES

Fifth-Year Student, Hufflepuff

A studious Hufflepuff, Adelaide
Oakes was raised by her uncle,
Rowland Oakes, after her father was
killed. Rowland is a brave adventurer
and a metal trader with goblins,
a profession not without risk.
Adelaide worries for his safety
when he goes missing.

SAMANTHA DALE

Fifth-Year Student, Ravenclaw

Samantha Dale is a descendant of
Marmaduke Gilbertus Dale, a famed
herbologist. She is obsessed with
her ancestors and researches
stories from her family history. She
has an impulsive, generally
disbelieving brother named
William, who sets out to prove her
wrong whenever he can and ends
up with cursed legs that have
turned into vegetables. Perhaps
you can help her reverse the curse?

OMINIS GAUNT

Fifth-Year Student, Slytherin

Ominis Gaunt is a bright, witty, and
sarcastic descendant of Salazar
Slytherin. He is best friends with the
Sallow twins, Sebastian and Anne.
He's been worried about Anne since
she was cursed and rendered unable
to return to school. While Sebastian is
obsessed with finding Anne a cure and
has been trying to enlist Ominis's help,
Ominis is uncomfortable with
Sebastian's inclination toward the
Dark Arts. Being loyal to his friends,
however, he reluctantly agrees to help
Sebastian despite his misgivings and
family history. Ominis uses his wand
to help him navigate, as he has been
blind since birth.

The Wizard's Field Guide

To help you keep track of your achievements—both in school and outside of Hogwarts—you are given a magical Field Guide. Every quest that you accept is monitored here, and you may tackle them at your own pace.

The Field Guide can be accessed almost anytime. Among its most useful functions is an interactive map of Hogwarts and its surroundings, which includes the village of Hogsmeade.

USING YOUR GUIDE
Make a point of checking your Field Guide regularly, especially for those Challenge Rewards. Alongside Talent Points, these can be a huge help.

Also indicated on the map are Floo Flames locations, providing shortcuts to areas where quests take place, a particularly useful vendor is stationed, or friends are in need of assistance.

As well as keeping track of your endeavors, the Field Guide rewards all efforts. Unique items are unlocked for slaying many foes, solving puzzles, and mastering broom flight. Your experience adds up to Talent Points, which you may allocate to personalize your magical performance.

SPELLS
0 / 10

DARK ARTS
0 / 10

CORE
0 / 16

STEALTH
0 / 4

ROOM OF REQUIREMENT
0 / 8

Spells to Get You Started

The Hogwarts professors waste little time acquainting you with essential charms for the road ahead. Fellow students also pass along incantations that serve them best.

In Defense Against the Dark Arts, Professor Hecat surprises the class with a demonstration of **LEVIOSO** (levitate objects). Although this may not seem like a powerful combat charm, it briefly disables and disorients the victim, allowing you time to land a few basic casts.

Professor Ronen finds a lighthearted use for **ACCIO** (pull objects), introducing you to the game of *Accio* Ball at Summoner's Court. Elsewhere in the world, casting *Accio* proves extremely handy for pulling levers, opening doors, or dragging foes toward you by their robes or armor for a pummeling.

Chinese Chomping Cabbages and Mandrakes are the **COMBAT PLANTS** first introduced by Professor Garlick in Herbology. These, alongside Venomous Tentacula, cause as much havoc as they do damage. Later on, in Professor Sharp's Potions class, you'll learn to prepare the healing brew Wiggenweld Potion.

To stock up on essential resources, you are encouraged to visit the nearby village of Hogsmeade. While shopping for seeds, recipes, and spell crafts, you are advised to stock up on **EDURUS POTIONS** (used for shielding) alongside Wiggenweld for healing.

WHO IS YOUR COMPANION?

SEBASTIAN SALLOW

Fifth-Year Student, Slytherin

Sebastian Sallow and his twin sister, Anne, live with their guardian, Uncle Solomon, in the hamlet of Feldcroft. Sebastian and his uncle have never seen eye to eye, but their relationship grew worse after Anne was cursed. Solomon has accepted Anne's situation as permanent and since Sebastian refuses to do the same, they are constantly at odds. Sebastian believes that by finding out who cursed Anne and studying the Dark Arts, he will find a cure. Anne is not only in constant physical pain, but she is also struggling with depression and unable to attend Hogwarts. While Sebastian's aims and goals are well-intentioned, he justifies acting questionably to achieve them. Sebastian is compelled by the idea that magic is a tool, rather than something innately good or evil.

Sebastian is intent on finding a cure for his sister, sometimes to the detriment of his friends. He is a powerful ally, but he has his own agenda.

NATSAI ONAI

Fifth-Year Student, Gryffindor

Natsai "Natty" Onai grew up in Africa, in Matabeleland, Zimbabwe, watching her mother, Mudiwa, use Divination to help protect their tribe from less-than-friendly neighbors. Her father was killed protecting her from local criminals when she was nine. Natty blames herself for her father's death. When Natty was ten, her mother accepted a position teaching at the magical school of Uagadou. Natty attended Uagadou for three years, where she learned how to become an Animagus (in the form of a gazelle). Before the start of Natty's fourth year, her mother accepted an offer to teach at Hogwarts. Natty has a special affinity for outsiders and those new to Hogwarts and will be one of your key allies during your time here.

Natty knows something is amiss at Hogwarts and Hogsmeade and is determined to discover the truth, even if it puts her in harm's way.

Hogsmeade Directory

The lively village is a key location for Main Quests and Side Quests alike. Vendors are introduced via entertaining plot developments, later becoming regular sources for supplies. There are many collectibles worth finding too, encouraging you to explore high and low.

TOMES AND SCROLLS
Enliven your Room of Requirement with spellcrafts (conjuration recipes) from Thomas Brown.

OLLIVANDERS—MAKERS OF FINE WANDS SINCE 382 BC
Customize your wand with help from Gerbold Ollivander, a true expert in his field.

J. PIPPIN'S POTIONS—POTIONS FOR ALL AILMENTS!
Your earliest long-distance Side Quest is set by Parry Pippin, who also sells essential products.

DOGWEED & DEATHCAP

Save time nurturing dangerous plants by visiting Beatrice Green, and stock up on seeds for later.

THE MAGIC NEEP

All your regular plants and seeds, for strength and healing, are offered by Timothy Teasdale.

BROOD & PECK

Ellie Peck sells beast by-products for crafting basic gear improvements at your magical loom. She will also help you safely rehome beasts in need of protection.

GLADRAGS WIZARDWEAR—CLOTHIER EXTRAORDINAIRE!

Enjoy a makeover with Augustus Hill, whose wizarding kit and clothing can mean a new you!

MADAM SNELLING'S TRESS EMPORIUM

Look terrific when attacking goblins and poachers after visiting hairdresser Calliope Snelling.

SPINTWITCHES SPORTING NEEDS

The enthusiastic Albie Weekes sells brooms and offers speed and handling enhancements.

The Three Broomsticks Inn

1 x butterbeer

1 x firewhisky

3 x butterbeers, extra foam

1 x gillywater,

2 x butterbeers

+butterbeer refill

The Three Broomsticks Inn is a fantastic place should you fancy yourself a butterbeer—or perhaps a spot to overhear some conversation. Drinks are served in tankards and enjoyed best next to the inn's cozy fire. Rumor has it this inn was one of the first establishments in all of Hogsmeade.

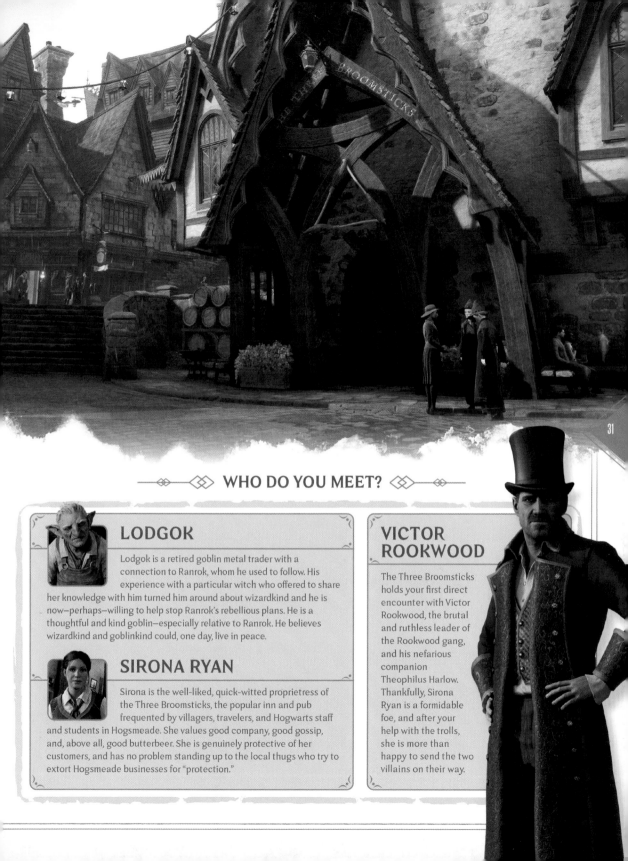

—◈—◇— WHO DO YOU MEET? —◇—◈—

LODGOK

Lodgok is a retired goblin metal trader with a connection to Ranrok, whom he used to follow. His experience with a particular witch who offered to share her knowledge with him turned him around about wizardkind and he is now—perhaps—willing to help stop Ranrok's rebellious plans. He is a thoughtful and kind goblin—especially relative to Ranrok. He believes wizardkind and goblinkind could, one day, live in peace.

SIRONA RYAN

Sirona is the well-liked, quick-witted proprietress of the Three Broomsticks, the popular inn and pub frequented by villagers, travelers, and Hogwarts staff and students in Hogsmeade. She values good company, good gossip, and, above all, good butterbeer. She is genuinely protective of her customers, and has no problem standing up to the local thugs who try to extort Hogsmeade businesses for "protection."

VICTOR ROOKWOOD

The Three Broomsticks holds your first direct encounter with Victor Rookwood, the brutal and ruthless leader of the Rookwood gang, and his nefarious companion Theophilus Harlow. Thankfully, Sirona Ryan is a formidable foe, and after your help with the trolls, she is more than happy to send the two villains on their way.

Troll Attack!

The Hogsmeade troll battle is your first major combat challenge. It teaches the importance of evading attacks while landing basic casts on target. *Protego* is also needed to deflect the hulking creature's heavyweight swipes.

During the encounter, the enraged creature pitches barrels and crates in your direction. While this is happening, you learn how to snatch a projectile mid-flight and hurl it straight back to the sender. This ancient magic throw leaves the troll stunned, briefly but long enough.

   The rampage is finally ended using the game-changing ancient magic finisher, a technique fueled by landing combos, or while absorbing damage. This inflicts colossal damage, overpowering the troll.

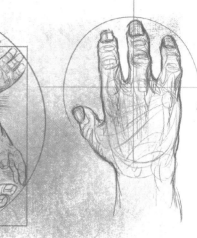

CALM VERSUS RAGE

Practice all your attack and evade techniques during these early stages of the adventure. Such combat basics are lifesavers in battles to come.

Dueling: Combo Timing and Shields

PROFESSOR DINAH HECAT

Defense Against the Dark Arts Professor

After graduating from Hogwarts at the top of her class, Dinah Hecat went on to have a successful career with the Ministry of Magic as an Unspeakable before becoming the Defense Against the Dark Arts professor. Strong-willed and direct, Hecat is known to be a strict but likable teacher. Being confined to a classroom often frustrates her, so she has developed a hands-on teaching method to satiate her desire for action.

Gryffindor's combat specialist, Lucan Brattleby, has tips on how to hone spell-casting. The trick is to link them into seamless, devastating, and utterly demoralizing combinations.

You can lift most average-size opponents into the air with *Levioso*, where they are entirely at the caster's mercy. Basic casts juggle them. Combos can be greatly extended using *Accio*.

Duels against enemies become more complex when Shields enter the equation. Some rivals project a protective aura, clearly visible and color-coded: Red, Violet, or Yellow.

Before such enemies can sustain damage, those shields must be targeted to break through. For example, *Levioso* versus Yellow Shields, *Accio* versus Violet Shields, and **INCENDIO** versus Red Shields.

VIOLET SHIELDS
Break through Violet Shields with Force spells like the Summoning Charm *Accio.*

The Dueling Club is a great way to master dueling and spell-casting. Stop by anytime to improve your skills. You'll battle against a training dummy (or other students!) and try out different combinations. Be sure to cast all your spells before the dummy lands.

THE

CROSSED WANDS

DUELING CLUB

You are hereby invited to join the exclusive and

– TOP SECRET –

Crossed Wands Dueling Club.

You will learn to defend yourself, attack your foe, and take a hit.

Bring your wand, and your nerve!

(Destroy this card after reading.)

PART 2:
THE FIRST TRIAL

Find the Book

Your success here relies on the Disillusionment Charm, which Sebastian Sallow imparts before the mission begins. Even while mostly invisible, move slowly to evade patrolling prefects outside the library and librarian Madam Scribner within.

Sebastian creates a noisy distraction, buying you time to swipe the Restricted Section key. Freestanding bookshelves provide the best cover to retreat, well out of Scribner's sight.

Once inside the Restricted Section, you'll need diversion tactics of your own to sneak past ghosts, casting basic spells that ricochet off walls. An encounter with Peeves forces Sebastian to retreat, leaving you to find the ancient magic portal leading to the Athenaeum.

SLOW IS SMOOTH

Stealth requires patience. Sometimes the fastest way through a section is to coolly observe before making your move, avoiding too many restarts.

I've not forgotten about our library venture—how did you fare?

If you're keen for some illicit spell practice, meet me outside the Defense Against the Dark Arts classroom. I know a discreet place near there.

Sebastian

The Athenaeum is where the book is held. To reach it, target switches located above arches to summon bridges. Other walkways rise into position if you stand on nearby pressure pads.

Use *Incendio*, *Accio*, and *Levioso* against the Pensieve sentries and sentinels in the high-vaulted rooms. Loot all the Athenaeum chests that contain high-level gear to equip later.

Pensieves:
Piecing the Story Together

❖

The secrets of the four Keepers are partly revealed through their memories, shared via Pensieves.

Professors Percival Rackham, Charles Rookwood, San Bakar, and Niamh Fitzgerald each have their own Pensieve. To gain access, you must perform the heroic acts laid out in their trials.

Their memories tell of a promising student, Isidora Morganach, whose misguided obsession with the curative potential of ancient magic leads to tragedy. Eventually you choose what to do with such harrowing knowledge, possibly impacting the future of the wizarding world.

ANCIENT MAGIC

Ancient magic is some of the most powerful magic in the wizarding world. It is the oldest, deepest magic and has been long forgotten by most wizards and witches, with only a few people able to see and harness its power. Ancient magic leaves traces, which you are able to see; the color of the trace depends on the nature of the magic.

The Pensieves play a major role in your understanding of the story and the part you play within it. Important memories are stored in vials, added to the basin. Each one pieces together the history surrounding ancient magic. After witnessing these vignettes, you gain possession of a curious artifact. The artifacts' importance is revealed in the closing chapter.

Herbology Class

Be sure to make use of potions, plants, and spell-casting in your adventures. They all help enormously, boosting attack strength, defensive power, and stealth capability.

Once learned, spells are yours forever, whereas potions, ingredients, and aggressive plant life need replenishing. This takes a bit of forethought when planning missions.

Nurturing Combat Plants is well worth the effort. Chomping Cabbages pursue and chew, Mandrake screams paralyze, and Venomous Tentacula cause poisonous damage.

To save time in the long run, buy Combat Plant seeds from Beatrice Green at Dogweed & Deathcap. It also works out significantly cheaper than full-grown specimens. The same goes for Parry Pippin, whose potions are convenient, but it is wiser to grow ingredients such as dittany for Wiggenweld.

Can be thrown at enemies!

Mandrake Root

ALSO KNOWN AS: Mandragora

APPEARANCE: Green leaves and brown stem

PROPERTIES:
Mandrake root and leaves are used in potion-making. Stewed Mandrake is a powerful restorative with the ability to cure those who have been cursed, petrified, or Transfigured.

DANGERS:
When pulled from the soil, fully matured Mandrakes emit a high-pitched scream that is fatal to those who hear it. A young Mandrake's scream is not fatal, though it can knock a person unconscious for several hours.

Remember to put cotton wool in your ears!

Simple to cultivate but takes time to grow

Chomping Cabbages

ALSO KNOWN AS:
Chinese Chomping Cabbages

APPEARANCE:
Green leaves, bulbous body

PROPERTIES:
Chomping Cabbages are a magical plant with a big appetite. They can eat many foods.

DANGERS:
Easy to lose a finger or two if you're not careful.

Dittany

ALSO KNOWN AS: Burning Bush

APPEARANCE: Dark green leaves and stem

PROPERTIES
Dittany is a powerful restorative and healing herb. It can be brewed for potion-making or eaten raw to cure light wounds. When crushed and placed over an open wound, it makes new skin grow at an accelerated rate.

RECIPE RESOURCES AND WHERE TO FIND THEM

Whether for your own gain or to assist the curious vendors inhabiting the Highlands, this list should make finding ingredients much easier. Of course, nobody can guarantee your safety while looking, but as a witch or wizard you are always magically well prepared!

ASHWINDER EGGS
Find these in rocky areas, near caves and along the coast— particularly those near abandoned campfires.

LACEWING FLIES
Search the open fields and meadows, especially bushes.

LEECHES (LEECH JUICE)
You'll spot these around water, near ponds and the sea.

LEAPING TOADSTOOLS
Forested areas are the logical place to bag such lively fungi.

HORKLUMPS
Sure to be in the region of vault, cave, or dungeon entrances.

Potions Class

During your first class, you will learn to brew two potions that will be useful to you throughout your time at Hogwarts. You will have procured the recipes for each during your trip to Hogsmeade, and here in Professor Sharp's classroom, you will use your new potion-making station to brew them.

Wiggenweld Potion

This is an invaluable potion for any student, but particularly for one pursued by unsavory characters. Wiggenweld is a powerful healing potion that can cure light injuries and knit together wounds. One of the key ingredients for Wiggenweld is **DITTANY SEEDS.** The seeds can be collected from a dittany plant, which you can grow in Herbology class.

Edurus Potion

Edurus Potion will be as useful to you as Wiggenweld, especially during a fight. Edurus is a protective potion that enhances your defense by covering you with a rocky, durable skin. You can brew this at your potion station when needed. The key ingredients you will need are Ashwinder eggs and **MONGREL FUR,** so make sure to stock up.

PROFESSOR AESOP SHARP

Potions Master

After graduating from Hogwarts, Aesop Sharp channeled his Defense Against the Dark Arts and potion-making prowess into a successful career as an Auror. He was severely injured and his partner killed after they failed to anticipate an ambush. The injury forced him into an early retirement from the Ministry and caused him to become even more vigilant. He applied for the position of Potions Master at Hogwarts—in part, hoping to use the resources at the school to treat his injury. Although he is generally respected by the students, his gruffness puts some off.

Early Side Quest Adventures

As your exploits become known around Hogwarts, various students begin reaching out for help. Alongside attractive rewards received for cooperation, you also gain experience points to increase your level. Plus, you get to know your way around the famous school.

In the "Flying Off the Shelves" Side Quest, Cressida Blume implores you to retrieve books that she has accidentally sent zipping around the library. This is an opportunity to perfect aiming accuracy with *Accio*, and gets you into the habit of scanning above your head for fluttering papers.

CRESSIDA BLUME

Fifth-Year Student, Gryffindor

Cressida Blume is known for her spell and charm inventions that backfire in spectacular fashion. She chides herself for not knowing her Latin well enough. She will ask you to help retrieve books and her diary, which she accidentally sent flying around the library.

During "Sacking Selwyn," acting on behalf of Hyacinth Olivier, your combat smarts are put to an early test in a battle against a gang of "Ashwinders," who are so named after serpents born of magical fire. Their leader Selwyn is a "named enemy" and as such is a highly valuable prize.

Similarly, a huge spider nicknamed **THE ABSCONDER** becomes the prime target of a Side Quest for Edgar Adley. In order to snatch a family heirloom from his friend's corpse, you'll learn how *Incendio* proves useful as a weapon (spiders hate fire!), and to sear through webbing.

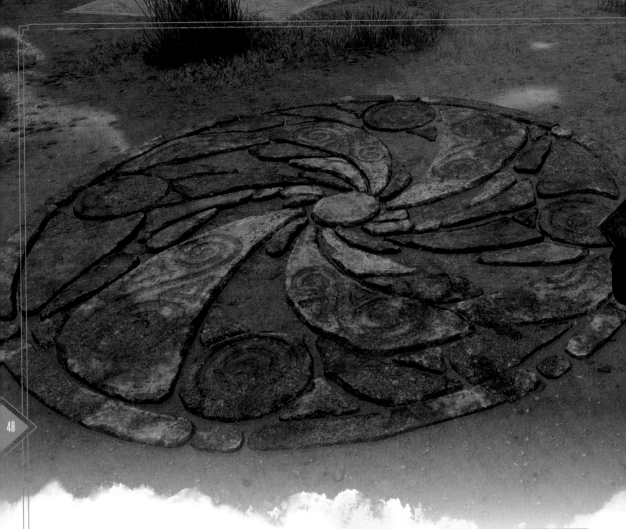

Merlin Trials

To unlock the Merlin Trials, you must first defend Nora Treadwell from Ashwinder scouts near Lower Hogsfield. After overhearing the commotion, you instinctively rush to Nora's aid.

Nora shows her gratitude by teaching you how to activate puzzles, sprinkling mallowsweet over the elaborately carved stone laid in the ground. Your first bag of mallowsweet is free and more can be bought at the Magic Neep in Hogsmeade, but you amass plenty while exploring.

Once you're initiated, the trial calls upon both knowledge and possession of specific magic spells. This may be a simple case of smashing small spheres of stone, or a combination of **DEPULSO** and *Accio* to maneuver much larger orbs. In some cases torches must be lit within a time limit, in others the glow of *Lumos* lures clouds of winged insects to flutter around crystalline rocks.

REWARDS
By solving these puzzles, you unlock more valuable slots in your inventory. Your experience points are boosted too.

49

Mallowsweet

Mallowsweet is a magical herb that can be used in a variety of ways. Its smoke is often inhaled by centaurs in their stargazing, it can be added to butterbeer for extra sweetness, and it is an ingredient in a number of potions.

Mallowsweet

Cache in the Castle

Hufflepuff student Arthur Plummly has found a treasure map in Professor Binns's office. If you share the same house, you'll strike up a conversation with him in the common room; otherwise, you're sure to encounter him in class.

ARTHUR PLUMMLY

Fifth-Year Student, Hufflepuff

Arthur Plummly is a cheerful boy who is well liked throughout Hogwarts. His complete lack of interest in anything of a competitive nature makes him rather unlike other boys his age. Arthur's Muggle mother instilled an overwhelming fear of beasts in all her children except Arthur, who loves creatures of every kind. He can be found with a map in his hand, asking you to join him on a treasure hunt.

The map shows clues in the form of four sketches. The sketches lead you past the Erumpent skeleton in the Defense Against the Dark Arts tower; into the Transfiguration Courtyard, passing the fountain and moving toward the courtyard tree; through the door leading to the bell tower; and up the staircase to where a painting of a snow-laden scene is mounted.

By casting *Revelio* on this painting, you'll see a sizable chest located behind it. Above the painting, embedded in the frame, is a handle. Whenever you see a handle, think *Accio*!

"Dissending" for Sweets

Garreth Weasley needs help locating dried Billywig stings for his Fizzing Whizbees—inspired beverage. You can find the shortest route to the Billywig stings' secret location in Honeydukes, which is some distance away, through the statue of the one-eyed witch.

The closest Floo Flames are in the Faculty Tower. The statue is in the third-floor corridor next to the Grand Staircase, which transports you to a labyrinth of rock-hewn tunnels.

You'll need to use **REPARO** several times to restore an elevator and various platforms. Where you see a feather icon etched into blocks, use the Levitation Spell *Levioso*. To raise the final platform,

the Summoning Charm *Accio* helps to dislodge an obstruction. The Fire-making Spell, *Incendio*, burns through all the cobwebs.

Thankfully there aren't any spiders! You only need *Incendio* again to get to the exit door. This takes you to the musty storage area below Honeydukes and to Garreth's Billywig stings.

BILLYWIG STINGS
A Billywig is a blue, magical insect whose sting is used in potion-making. The sting can cause a person to levitate.

Brother's Keeper

You become the bearer of bad news as you follow up on a missing person in Upper Hogsfield. Claire Beaumont's brother, Bardolph, was last seen at the ruins at the edge of the Forbidden Forest where it meets the North Ford Bog.

When you get there, **INFERI** (reanimated corpses) are patrolling the place. One is wearing a wool sweater, matching the description of the sweater once knitted for Bardolph. Regrettably, you must slay every last one of them—yes, including poor Bardolph. Helpfully, the Inferi are weakened with fire.

Exactly how you explain events to Madam Beaumont is up to you. There may be a way of telling the truth without being too harsh, but you may consider it best to be direct.

I hate that I'm afraid. But there's no going back. I seem to have mastered two of the curses so far. But I've had to pledge to do their bidding if I'm to learn more.

I can't let them see my fear. They're already whispering behind my back.

I've been told not to trust Dark wizards, but I can't stop until I have enough magic to protect Claire, myself, and all of Upper Hogsfield.

Bardolph

Breaking Camp

Y ou must deal with more trouble for Claire
Beaumont, the Upper Hogsfield vendor.
Ranrok's Loyalist goblins are disrupting trade
routes, preventing Claire from doing business.

Show the goblins who's boss by marching on their
nearby camps, practicing the use of basic casts and
simple combos. The Levitation Spell *Levioso* is
especially strong against these low-level grunts.

   Follow the markers to both locations. Do your
work, and head back to Madam Beaumont. You may
pretend that this was extraordinarily difficult, or act
like it was no trouble at all.

The Lost Astrolabe

Grace Pinch-Smedley wants you to retrieve her family's astrolabe from the bottom of the Black Lake. Although the mission sounds as though it might be dangerous, there is almost certainly something in this for you. Besides, Grace has a lot of faith in you.

Her precise calculations are marked a ways offshore, where the water is coldest.

In the end, this is short but satisfying work. Grace is hugely appreciative, which means a lot. Also, you now have the knack for diving. Who knows what else you'll find!

GRACE PINCH-SMEDLEY

Fourth-Year Student, Slytherin

Grace Pinch-Smedley is a pleasant young lady who is seemingly well liked by all and appears destined to become a prefect before long. Grace descends from the Bath Pinch-Smedleys. For various familial reasons she will explain, she is not allowed to enter the Black Lake, so she needs your help to retrieve a lost family heirloom.

Carted Away

Not too far from the Black Lake in Lower Hogsfield, a goblin trader called Arn reports that his carts have been stolen and, along with them, his dear paintings. He suggests that Ranrok's Loyalists are responsible. Their camp is roughly southwest in the Hogwarts Valley.

The carts are enchanted and will find their own way back once rescued. However, the goblins are large in number, well organized, and some are using shields as protection.

Your first gambit should be to cast the Disillusionment Charm and remain undetected, sneaking up on guards to perform the Body-Bind Curse **PETRIFICUS TOTALUS**. If all goes well, it's time to turn up the heat!

Use ancient magic to hurl explosive barrels, doubly effective against Red Shields. **CONFRINGO** (Blasting Curse) and **EXPELLIARMUS** (Disarming Charm) open their bearers to attack. The Levitation Spell, *Levioso*, may be the only yellow-coded spell in your arsenal for now, but it is quite effective.

The Summoning Charm, *Accio*, clears the way for the carts to return to Arn, who is overwhelmed with gratitude.

Troll Control

Alexandra Ricketts's bright idea to domesticate a troll to defend her hamlet backfires. **Your task is to bring matters under control, which means besting the creature in battle.**

If you attempt this early in your adventure, you'll learn to crush larger foes the hard way. Watch out for the swing of his arm and dodge smartly out of reach before he takes a swipe. Have the Shield Charm, *Protego*, ready to parry rocks and use ancient magic to fling them back.

This troll encounter is as hair-raising as it gets and takes some time to complete, but it is very satisfying.

Kidnapped Cabbage

This Side Quest could be the first time you'll find yourself surrounded, which is challenging. It involves clearing two camps: one a pack of poachers, the other Ranrok's Loyalists.

Shielded enemies are common by now, so equip a range of spells to disrupt them and counter. The pack includes an Animagus and Executioner, who you'll need to subdue using the Levitation Spell, *Levioso*, and Disarming Charm, *Expelliarmus*. Regular foes fall to basic casts, but the Shield Charm, *Protego*, and Stunning Spell, *Stupefy*, do help.

It is best to approach the Loyalist camp from the north. This puts you behind the main tent, out of sight, buying time for an opening salvo before the goblins discover you're there. Your Levitation Spell helps to disrupt attacks. Use Shield Charms to stop swift-moving goblin assassins in their tracks.

E-Vase-Ive Maneuver

You may find this the most straightforward Side Quest on your journey, but it is also fun. *Revelio* is your go-to spell, to locate twenty rather attractive vases before you shatter them with basic casts.

Althea Twiddle in Irondale talks of her husband Greville's obsession with a local puzzle. The location is to the southwest, where a Combat Arena is marked. It's a short hop via broom. Simply vanquish those twenty vicious vases, practicing your aim while doing so.

Mrs. Twiddle is perfectly happy to learn that her dearly departed was right about his hunch, and ready with her reward. If you are feeling brave, however, you can also approach the statue in the center of the Arena to enter into a Combat Challenge against waves of merciless foes!

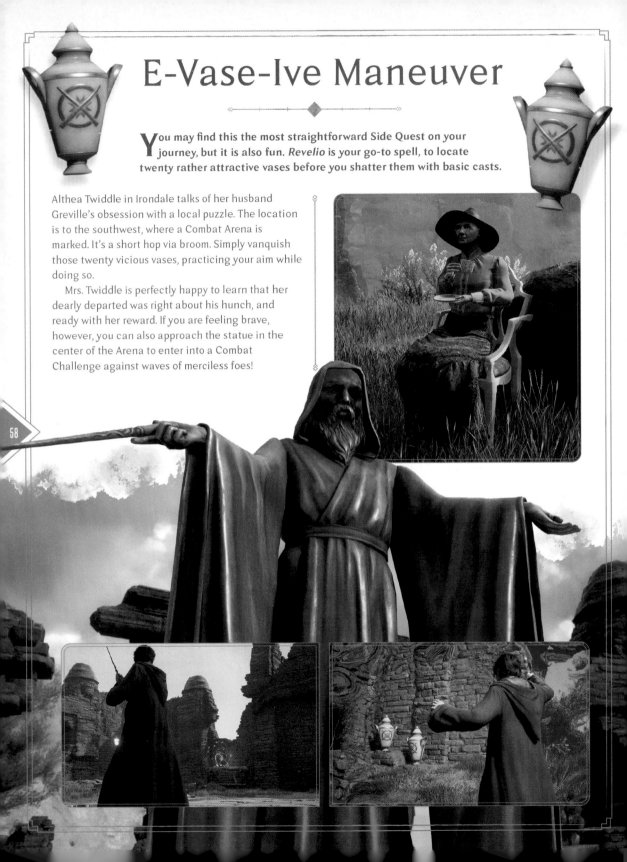

DIRICAWLS

A Diricawl is a plump-bodied, flightless but magical bird, known commonly to Muggles as the (apparently) extinct dodo. It uses an ability similar to Apparating—being able to disappear and reappear at will—making it very hard to catch.

Birds of a Feather

Soon after passing the First Trial, you acquire the nab-sack and the Disillusionment Charm. Both are needed to complete this heartwarming Side Quest for Marianne Moffett.

There's a particular Diricawl named Gwyneira to retrieve from a cliffside den close to the South Poidsear Floo Flames. Arriving via the Floo Flames also allows you to wait until nighttime, which is the only opportunity you get to snaffle the beautiful snow-white Diricawl for Miss Moffett.

Once at the location, approach under the cover of Disillusionment and wait until Gwyneira joins her flock. This takes a while. Be sure to have *Levioso* equipped and the nab-sack at the ready. Diricawls vanish and flee when disturbed, so have patience until Gwyneira's name appears.

By immobilizing her with *Levioso*, Gwyneira is unable to disappear and much easier to rescue.

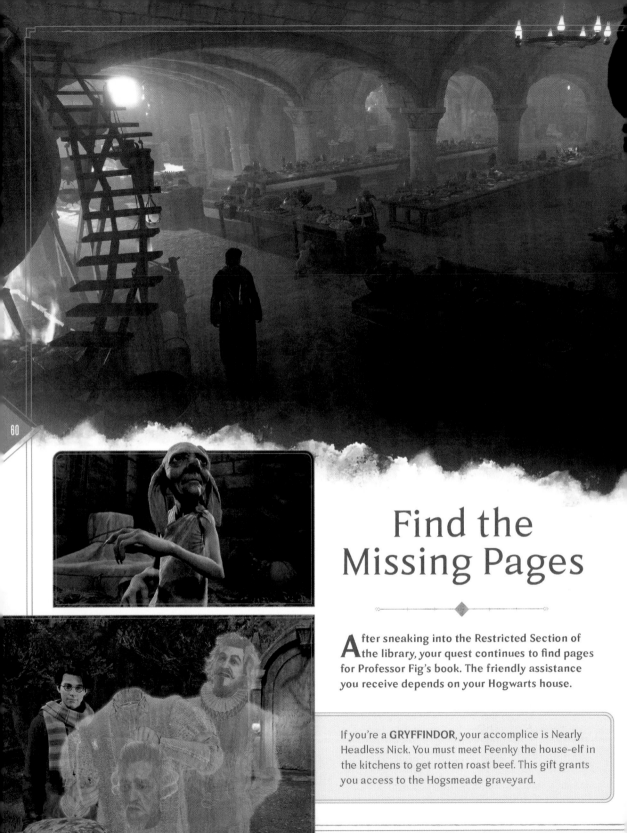

Find the Missing Pages

After sneaking into the Restricted Section of the library, your quest continues to find pages for Professor Fig's book. The friendly assistance you receive depends on your Hogwarts house.

If you're a **GRYFFINDOR**, your accomplice is Nearly Headless Nick. You must meet Feenky the house-elf in the kitchens to get rotten roast beef. This gift grants you access to the Hogsmeade graveyard.

For **HUFFLEPUFFS**, the portrait of Eldritch Diggory requests that you talk to his great-niece, ex-Auror Helen Thistlewood, who suggests going to Azkaban.

RAVENCLAW students head to the Owlery in search of clues on how to retrieve a family wand for Gerbold Ollivander.

For **SLYTHERIN** students, the Black family house-elf, Scrope, directs you to a secret grotto.

Scrope knows about that book you found. Is it missing something?

Scrope does not believe it is safe to speak out in the open.

Scrope has left another note across the bridge, among the circle of rocks.

Take care.
Tell no one about this.

After performing one of these duties, the ghost of Richard Jackdaw picks up the trail.

Jackdaw's Rest
(The Forbidden Forest)

Your first major excursion is deliciously spooky. Not only are you helping a (quite charming) ghost to locate its skeletal remains, the cadaver lies in the dismal depths of a colossal cave.

The spirit of Richard Jackdaw guides you into the Forbidden Forest, but only so far. Your instructions are to look out for three helpful landmarks leading you to the cave: a bridge, waterfall, and lake. Use this opportunity to highlight the Main Quest location on the map, which provides a waypoint to follow. In fact, this is sensible practice from here on out.

With the route highlighted, turn right before the waterfall between towering tree trunks. Outside Jackdaw's tomb there is a birdbath. It reveals a secret entrance after hearing the password provided by Jackdaw.

Before heading inside, you must first battle a gang of Loyalist goblins that are lying in wait. They are cunning and Red-Shielded, so employ the Disarming Charm, *Expelliarmus*, and the Fire-making Spell, *Incendio*, to defeat them.

Within the cave, there are two recurring puzzles: doors locked using three timed switches, and floating platforms that must be deliberately positioned and repositioned to make progress.

The trick with switches is to blast them, identifying those that have the fastest countdown. Casting *Revelio* highlights where all three switches are located, but you do need to be fast on the draw.

With the floating platforms, use the compass to remember which areas you have explored. It is easy to become disoriented otherwise.

There are treasure chests throughout the cave. Spend time investigating every crooked trail marked on the map. Be prepared for Thornback spiders, which are weak against *Expelliarmus* and *Incendio*. The latter is especially effective against the matriarch, who writhes on her back when scorched. Use ancient magic to finish her off.

POWER OF THE MIND

There are puzzle elements to many obstacles faced on your journey. Think logically and practically and you will succeed ... sooner or later.

My dearest Anne,

Well done! You solved my puzzle. I knew you were a kindred spirit and the only one with whom I could truly share my adventures. Meet me at the edge of the Forbidden Forest as soon as you can and I will show you the map that I mentioned. There is no telling where it will lead us. I found it on pages that Peeves ripped from a secret book and no one else seems to be able to find. I haven't any idea what lies ahead, but I am glad to know I shall share my future with you.

This is only the beginning.

Richard

P.S. I am terribly glad you found this, as I would have gone on alone if you did not. And what fun would that be?

Jackdaw's remains lie in a chamber guarded by relentless Pensieve Sentinels and Protectors. Disarming them buys time to focus fire on other targets.

Gobs of Gobstones

Go and meet Zenobia Noke in the Defense Against the Dark Arts tower. Zenobia's humorless classmates have confiscated her Gobstones. These are scattered in high places all around Hogwarts, where tiny Zenobia cannot reach. Luckily, you hold the secret to their recovery!

Zenobia begs that you seek out the missing Gobstones since you know the Summoning Charm, *Accio*, and she doesn't. This task is something you can manage while completing most other Quests and Assignments around school. Whenever a Gobstone is close by, your avatar mentions that this may be the case, and you need only cast *Revelio* to investigate the walls and rafters.

A Friend In Deed

Sirona Ryan asks you to come to the Three Broomsticks in Hogsmeade. She asks that you help her friend, Dorothy Sprottle, to collect horklumps for use in her Wiggenweld Potion.

You may already have foraged armfuls of horklumps while on your travels, in which case, hand them over. Failing that, the second part of Sirona's Quest surely delivers the supplies. In Horklump Hollow, a short flight away, you also find letters that Aidan was bringing to Sirona—letters that provide a glimpse into Sirona's life as a student at Hogwarts.

The cavern also hides a massive troll. Before confronting this monster, be sure to blast open a hidden room to your left as soon as you enter. It is crawling with Devil's Snare, but you can light a torch to keep it at bay. There are also many Moonstone rocks here to mine.

As for the troll, this one is more inclined to rush you than most. Your Dodge Roll comes in extremely handy. Keep your wits about you, keep up with the barrage of basic casts, drop ancient magic finishers at every opportunity, and hurl everything in the room at him!

Follow the Butterflies

At the Three Broomsticks, Clementine Willardsey is wondering about butterflies hovering near the Forbidden Forest. She is too scared of the forest to figure out why for herself, so you kindly offer to report back. The North Hogwarts Region Floo Flames take you there fast.

From the Forbidden Forest entrance, follow the butterflies upstream toward a spider's lair. You can claim your prize from the chest surrounded by the butterflies without starting a fight.

However, quarreling with spiders is good combat experience for a trainee wizard or witch.

Summoner's Court: Match 1

After learning *Accio* from Professor Ronen, your fellow students seek to impress one another at the Summoner's Court. Meet them outside on the lawn when you're ready.

Leander Prewett is first to test your mettle, raising the stakes with bumpers as obstacles. To achieve victory, focus on two main points: line of sight and effect of velocity against an opponent's stationary ball. Leander is, you will note, quite poor at this.

Like all sports, Summoner's Court requires practice. If you can judge distance between bumpers and gauge the momentum required to bash a rival's

effort off the board, these simple skills will be the building blocks of a glorious career.

Trouncing Leander proves you are the real deal, ready to face summoning champ Samantha Dale.

ABRAHAM RONEN

Charms Professor

Abraham Ronen is always at ease with his students. He considers the act of helping young students grow as people to be just as important as the subject of Charms. Ronen was tutored by a rather austere father before and during his years at Hogwarts. This resulted in Professor Ronen developing a passion for games of all forms and making a game of his studies—a practice he incorporates into his teaching today. He particularly adores Gobstones.

LEANDER PREWETT

Fifth-Year Student, Gryffindor

Leander Prewett is a blustery Gryffindor who never misses an opportunity to proclaim his house pride, much to the annoyance of the rest of his school. His bravado is really a mask for his insecurities about living up to the Gryffindor ideals of courage and heroism.

THE GIFT OF FLIGHT

Learning to fly a broom transforms your potential to explore. Distances are covered so much faster. Merlin Trials and more are spied from the sky.

Flying Class

Grab a broom for your first lesson in flying!

Madam Kogawa has two rudimentary exercises to ease you into it: Fly through three rings to get a feel for directional control, and complete one circuit of Hogwarts to experience faster speeds.

You may be happy with your first attempts, but Everett Clopton encourages you to fly even faster.

He invites you to fly with him on a gust-busting chase around the school, leaning forward for aerodynamic effect, rattling Hufflepuff common room windows, and circling the Owlery. Yes, this does get you into big trouble with Madam Kogawa, but she is secretly impressed.

HOGWARTS
SCHOOL OF
WITCHCRAFT & WIZARDRY

Dear Madam Kogawa,

Marvelous news that you will be joining the faculty at Hogwarts as our new Flying instructor.

I daresay our work together at Hogwarts will be less eventful than our time near Yokohama Harbor though one never knows.

I shall look forward to seeing you soon. If you have any questions in the meantime, please do not hesitate to send me an owl.

Warm regards,

Matilda Weasley

EMBER DASH BROOM

The perfect broom for those with a fiery temperament

Cost

PURCHASE   PREVIEW BROOM

Next, hurry to Spintwitches in Hogsmeade to browse finely crafted brooms. The Ember Dash costs 4 Gold, which can be earned by selling a few unused items. Once flown, you will never look back.

CHIYO KOGAWA

Flying Professor

Madam Kogawa attended school at Mahoutokoro and eventually worked for the Japanese Ministry of Magic, which is how she met Professor Weasley and was recruited to join Hogwarts. Thought to be a generally affable person and teacher, Kogawa becomes another person when teaching flying and disciplining students. A bad experience in her tryouts for the Toyohashi Tengu Quidditch team taught her a valuable lesson about honor and trust, and she values both highly. Now, any foul sportsmanship on a student's part will have them banned from the match quicker than you can say "Quaffle."

In the Shadow of the Undercroft

Sebastian Sallow has a secret he'd like to share. Meet him at the foot of the stairs leading to the Defense Against the Dark Arts classroom, in the Hall of Herodiana.

He leads you to an ornate cabinet, which is a portal to the Undercroft. This place is unknown even to Hogwarts professors. Sebastian reveals his fascination with dangerous spells, such as the Blasting Curse, *Confringo*. He urges you to embrace its power, which you cautiously accept.

   In battle, *Confringo* is reliably punishing against Red-Shielded enemies, and especially spiders. Its ability to set distant targets burning also helps to solve puzzles and Merlin Trials to come.

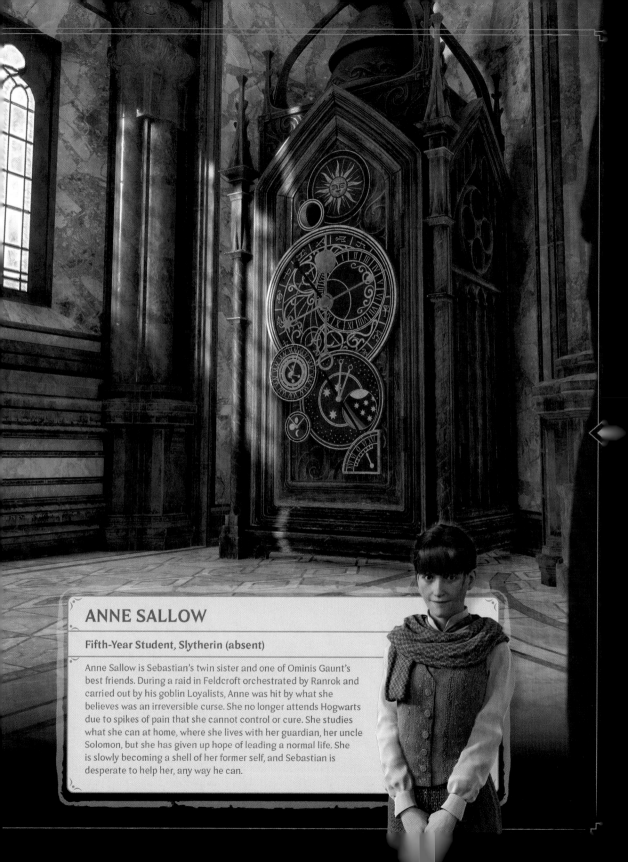

ANNE SALLOW

Fifth-Year Student, Slytherin (absent)

Anne Sallow is Sebastian's twin sister and one of Ominis Gaunt's best friends. During a raid in Feldcroft orchestrated by Ranrok and carried out by his goblin Loyalists, Anne was hit by what she believes was an irreversible curse. She no longer attends Hogwarts due to spikes of pain that she cannot control or cure. She studies what she can at home, where she lives with her guardian, her uncle Solomon, but she has given up hope of leading a normal life. She is slowly becoming a shell of her former self, and Sebastian is desperate to help her, any way he can.

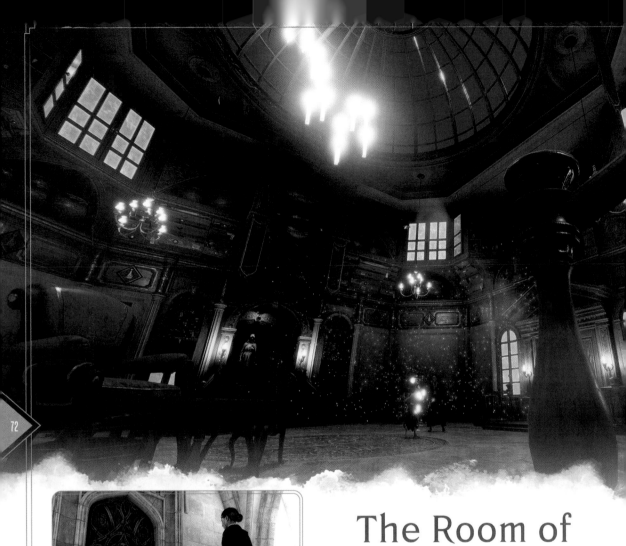

The Room of Requirement

Professor Weasley asks that you meet her in the seventh-floor corridor at Hogwarts. Here, you enter the Room of Requirement, at first under the guise of the Room of Hidden Things.

While browsing the Room of Requirement, Professor Weasley teaches **EVANESCO**, a spell that vanishes certain objects. You meet Deek the house-elf and learn what Moonstone can be used for, all leading to the grand restructuring of the room as your private retreat and workplace.

Inside the Room of Requirement is a Desk of Description, to identify unknown items of clothing and accessories. Professor Weasley also tells you about magical recipes called spellcrafts, which you can use to personalize a locale.

MOONSTONE

Moonstone is a white, milky gemstone that shines brightly. It is used in numerous potions, including love potions and the Draught of Peace. It can be bought powdered or whole or acquired through disappearing objects using *Evanesco*.

You need Moonstone to conjure and transfigure tables for brewing potions and growing plants. This can be bought at Tomes and Scrolls in Hogsmeade, but Moonstone crystals are scattered all over the Highlands. Vanishing unwanted objects with *Evanesco* also produces Moonstone.

Next, you'll conjure wall hangings and artwork, and room decorations that include clocks and ornate folding screens. Their appearance can be modified, changing style, color, and size. You can also affect the room's architecture, including balconies and floors.

You can obtain new spellcrafts by completing quests and finding chests that are littered around the world. Most are easy to spot, with something modest inside. The rare kinds—larger and more decorative—you really need to poke around to discover.

The Room of Requirement grows to accommodate the increasing range of conjurations in your collection as you become gradually more self-sufficient. For a finishing touch, Deek shows how to change the room's ambience between cool and moonlit, natural and earthy, warm and cozy, or dark and mysterious.

DEEK

Hogwarts House-Elf

Deek has been serving at Hogwarts for a long time, seen thousands of students come and go, and had a wide variety of jobs. He has always been a genuinely well-liked and social house-elf and, unlike most of the other house-elves serving at Hogwarts, allows himself to be seen by the students. Prior to working at Hogwarts, he worked for a merciless, evil poacher who forced Deek to capture beasts. When the poacher died, Deek was one of the lucky ones who got sent to Hogwarts. Deek is happy to help you use the nab-sack to rescue beasts and save them from all the poachers in the area.

A Demanding Delivery

Parry Pippin at J. Pippin's Potions asks you to deliver Invisibility Potions to a tricky customer. This would be Fatimah Lawang of Keenbridge, way down south in the Hogwarts Valley.

It is best to travel by broom, if you already have one. Then save time on the way back by returning via the West Hogsmeade Floo Flames. Parry's modest cash reward will buy some potions.

The Daedalian Keys

Nellie Oggspire alerts you to the flutter of enchanted keys that fly around Hogwarts. These are charmed to protect locked cabinets. Your fast reflexes soon reveal why.

From her spot in the Transfiguration Courtyard, Nellie asks you to find sixteen winged keys. Once located, the keys draw your attention to the whereabouts of their respective cabinet. All you need to do is give chase.

Your search begins in the Astronomy Tower, where a key whizzes to a nearby classroom. Slap the key into place—with good timing—to find a token etched with your house crest.

The tokens belong in the house chest in your common room. Catch them all for a prize.

Talent Points and Taking Stock

◇—————◆—————◇

It has been quite a journey until this point, but you are surely gaining independence—not only as a Hogwarts student, but as a player. Every task accepted boosts your Experience, which can be as grand as crushing a troll in Hogsmeade or being kind to students in need.

This is where the adventure turns toward large-scale matters, greater mysteries, and the pursuit of key adversaries. Although you remain at the center of it all, powerful allies now make themselves known. Your road ahead stretches from forest to dale, coast to coast.

You escort Professor Fig to the Map Chamber beneath Hogwarts, where he lays the book from the Restricted Section on a pedestal. This transforms

the floor area into shimmering representations of locations around Hogwarts. Much greater tasks now lie ahead.

By now, you will have learned a wide range of spells that can be used in combat: *Levioso, Accio, Depulso, Confringo, Expelliarmus,* and *Incendio.* You may also acquire **GLACIUS** and **DIFFINDO** at this point, through assignments for Madam Kogawa and Professor Sharp. Your exploits may have tipped your Experience above Level 10, a milestone that unlocks Talent Points in your Field Guide.

Professor Rackham explains how your enhanced abilities attune you to ancient magic. This is related to your Talent Points in the game. Consider spending these Talent Points ahead of Professor Rackham's Trial, which takes place at San Bakar's Tower in the North Ford Bog.

Under Spells, *Levioso* mastery levitates multiple foes. In the Stealth category, the Sense of Secrecy Talent makes you harder to detect under Disillusionment. The Core enhancement, basic cast mastery, boosts the recharge rate for all spells.

As Rackham resolutely points out, the trial must be faced entirely alone, since only those channeling ancient magic can solve the puzzles—and, one most sincerely hopes, survive.

TAILORING YOUR TALENTS

Every witch or wizard develops a style that is unique. Talents let you boost the effectiveness of spells and skills, including those of the Dark Arts.

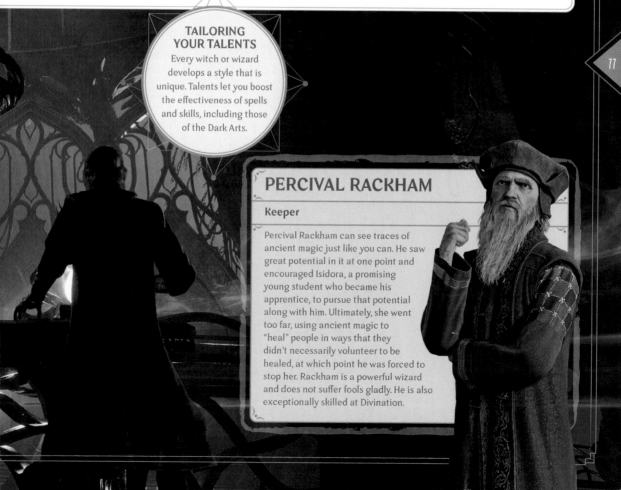

PERCIVAL RACKHAM

Keeper

Percival Rackham can see traces of ancient magic just like you can. He saw great potential in it at one point and encouraged Isidora, a promising young student who became his apprentice, to pursue that potential along with him. Ultimately, she went too far, using ancient magic to "heal" people in ways that they didn't necessarily volunteer to be healed, at which point he was forced to stop her. Rackham is a powerful wizard and does not suffer fools gladly. He is also exceptionally skilled at Divination.

Percival Rackham's Trial

Professor Fig guides you through the approach to San Bakar's Tower, guarded by goblins. Fig teaches you *Petrificus Totalus* under cover of Disillusionment—sneaky, and extremely useful.

After investigating the first reservoir, a portal appears to reveal a broken bridge. The first puzzle involves crossing into a dimension where the intact version exists.

Percival Rackham's Trial introduces the effects of the reservoirs on the environment. These effects are altered when passing through portals—objects that you spy on one side are not always found on the other or take a different form. No need to panic, just observe to spot

where any differences might help to solve the puzzle.

You must also think about strategic placement of moving platforms, guiding them into place with *Accio*. Be sure to backtrack and inspect areas using *Revelio*, to expose treasure chests or any helpful items that you may have missed.

Along the way you will encounter Pensieve Protectors and smaller Pensieve Sentinels. You can launch the latter to their doom using *Depulso*, and all

of them can be disarmed with *Expelliarmus*. Use Dodge Roll to avoid being surrounded, and watch for where leaping Sentinels land!

Your final opponent is an immense Pensieve Guardian, whose stomps create shock waves and who occasionally attempts to swat you with a gigantic orb. *Expelliarmus* is successful here too, buying time to build power for ancient magic finishers that crush the Guardian's defenses.

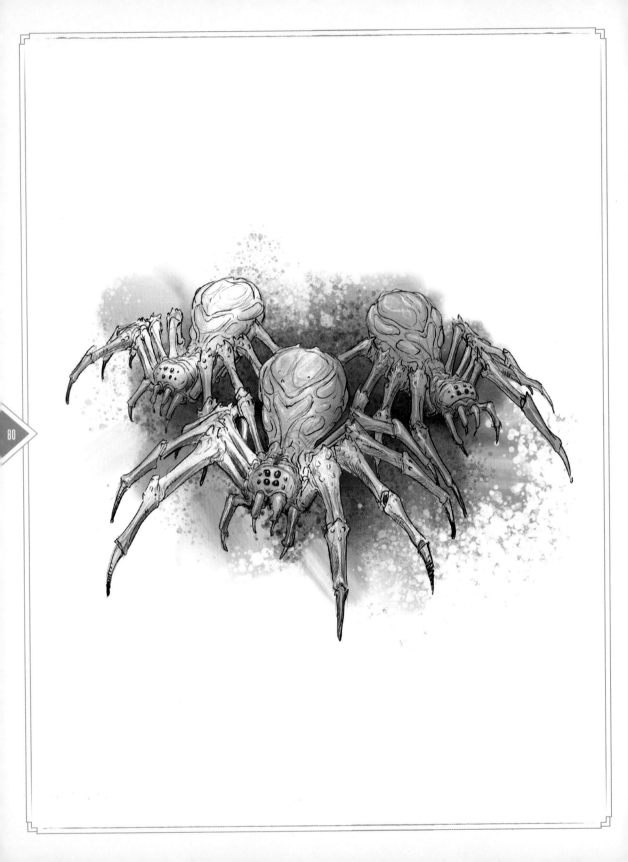

PART 3:
THE SECOND TRIAL

The Helm of Urtkot

The experience of completing your first trial is a confidence boost for challenges to come. Events leading up to the Keepers' Trials with Professor Rackham also illustrate how to structure your progress. Pay attention to letters arriving by Owl Post, which all point to important next steps. These are added to your list of quests and assignments that carry you through the adventure. Such quests continue to be instructional, even at this stage.

Sirona at the Three Broomsticks puts you in contact with a goblin named Lodgok, who has knowledge of Ranrok's plans. He'd like something in exchange for that info, however. Not far from Hogsmeade, a witch's tomb holds a prized goblin artifact: the Helm of Urtkot.

This tomb resembles a mine with rock-hewn rooms and wooden supports. The relic is locked away behind a series of doors, each one activated by glowing moths lured into curious mechanisms. Casting *Lumos* is the key.

You only need one moth to release the first door, but more moths are hidden or otherwise obscured for the doors that follow. Use *Accio* and *Incendio* to solve the more complex riddles, but you will need to cast *Depulso* to swivel floor-mounted keys that raise platforms.

You will also encounter Inferi. Once struck by fire, these creatures are vulnerable to all subsequent attacks.

Treat the tomb as a training ground for many helpful skills. One tucked-away room has a chest accessed via a bridge of bones that casting *Accio* helps to assemble. A withered rope is snapped by a spell that also proves extremely useful amid a crowd of Inferi.

The final moth puzzle is tricky. Pay attention to the nature of platforms raised by the switch.

In the closing Ashwinder camp battle against a forest troll and an Ashwinder assassin, being quick on your feet and with your spell selections gives you a strong foundation for countless battles to come.

SHEDDING NEW LIGHT
You encounter several puzzles involving luminous moths, which you must seek out before guiding them into place. They are linked to substantial rewards.

ARRESTO MOMENTUM

Take the Floo Flames to Keenbridge for Madam Kogawa's second assignment. This is a sightseeing journey around old Keenbridge Tower and nearby geological wonder the Spires.

Once in the vicinity of the old tower, waypoint markers plot your course as you admire the views. It is a trial of confidence in handling, following and popping balloons at

each location and tracing fast-flowing waters upstream. Use speed boost bubbles for added speed.

Northwest of the tower, on the hillside beyond stone ruins, are the Spires' distinctive rock formations. Weave between these, drifting tightly around corners to target the waypoints. Madam Kogawa waits for you in her study when you return, fresh-faced and windswept.

DESCENDO

Before you learn how to cast **DESCENDO** from Professor Onai, you must first complete her assignment.

Professor Onai is found working diligently in her Divination Classroom, and gladly teaches you *Descendo*. She also asks you to peer into your future, challenging your self-perception.

Casting *Descendo* causes objects to fall and slam into the ground with such force as to create a shock wave. It is extremely effective against foes of broadly human stature.

Depulso, which launches objects and opponents backward, may be field-tested during the "Helm of Urtkot" quest. It upsets Ashwinder assassins, but not river trolls. Their mucus can be retrieved during the Ashwinder camp battle or purchased from J. Pippin's Potions in Hogsmeade.

Attend Beasts Class

Professor Howin's class takes place outdoors. It is a short lesson, introducing basic care of magical beasts. In this case, keeping Puffskeins and Kneazles happy with a brush and feed.

BAI HOWIN

Beasts and Magical Creatures Professor

Bai Howin has a respect for beasts but sees them first and foremost as useful resources for wizardkind. An experience with an Occamy left her in awe of beasts, and she loathes poachers who would waste them for Galleons. In her mind, beasts are to be valued for what they can provide for wizardkind: protective clothing, potion ingredients—even wand cores. It is her mission to ensure that the next generation of witches and wizards understands this.

You befriend Poppy Sweeting, whose affinity with beasts is really extraordinary. Poppy also notices the care with which you treat the Puffskeins and Kneazles, soon gaining their trust.

Right after class, Poppy introduces you to Highwing the Hippogriff, whom you tame by brushing, feeding, and bowing to the beast. The nervous Hippogriff was rescued from Rookwood's poachers. Now Poppy aims to track them down and put an end to their nefarious plans.

Poppy's Relationship Quests are always eventful and can be quite dangerous!

Dear Professor Howin,

I would be more than happy to take any excess Puffskein hair from you. I could collect it when I next make a delivery to the castle. Sounds as if you have plenty for your classroom needs?

Perhaps you might even have time for a cup of tea? A little bird told me that you once encountered an Occamy. I can't say I'd mind hearing about that!

I once encountered a young Welsh Green when I was collecting toad hide in the west. 'Course, it could've been a baby Wyvern. Hard to tell at that age.

Anyway, not for the faint of heart, is it, this life with magical beasts?

Looking forward to your response,

Ellie Peck

POPPY SWEETING

Fifth-Year Student, Hufflepuff

Poppy Sweeting is a compassionate girl with a big heart for creatures. She believes they have far more redeeming values than people, something she learned at a young age. Her parents are poachers and she grew up in poacher camps, a past she struggles with. Given the choice, she much prefers the company of creatures to people and can appear reserved as a result. She is currently estranged from her parents and lives with her grandmother when not at school. She is terribly bright and has an unmistakable air of independence about her.

"Mer-ky" Depths

Hogwarts's boathouse docks are a short hop on your broom to where Nerida Roberts waits. Nerida aspires to become the first liaison to merpeople, working at the Ministry of Magic.

Unable to swim, Nerida needs you to fetch a Mermish artifact from the lake. You could swim to the dive spot, but it is faster to skim the water by broom and drop down in style.

WHAT ARE YOU HIDING?
Cobwebs are found in many ancient chambers and, a lot of the time, hide something useful. Burn them away to reveal modest treasures, new pathways, and gadgets required to solve the puzzle at hand.

You emerge in an airtight chamber, where a moth-activated door stands between you and the prize. Two of the moths are behind cobwebs, which *Incendio* or *Confringo* can consume. When you return, Nerida thanks you for contributions to wizardkind and merpeople relations.

The Man Behind the Moons

Caretaker Gladwin Moon is being plagued by Demiguise statues that have been placed all over the grounds. Can you help him get to the bottom of this cruel practical joke?

Meet Gladwin near the Reception Hall. He talks of Demiguise statues clutching moons that must be collected after dark. Retrieve all the moons to expose the person guilty of plonking them around Hogwarts and neighboring hamlets (much to Gladwin's annoyance).

To begin the search, Gladwin teaches the Unlocking Charm, **ALOHOMORA**, which can be used to open a door to the Prefect Chambers and Hospital Wing. Use *Revelio* and the Disillusionment Charm to sneak around.

After this quest, use the Wait function of Floo Flames to hunt Demiguise statues by night. Nine moons prompt Gladwin to teach *Alohomora* II for Level 2 locks. More detective work grants *Alohomora* III for Level 3 locks. Bag the moons as soon as you see them—there are lots.

The Prestigious Writings of
GLADWIN MOON

Dear Diary,

Each day it becomes more difficult to put on a brave face as I care for my beloved Hogwarts.

Daily, it seems, I stumble upon yet another Demiguise statue. Who is behind this? Whom have I wronged to such extent that they must now torture me with these foul things?

I despair. Ever since I encountered that horrible creature in Hogsmeade, I have been unable to sleep. I fear I am not only distracted from my duties by these blasted statues, but I may also be looking rather worse for wear without my requisite eight to nine hours of slumber.

I must remain steadfast. If I falter, to whom will the students look for guidance in these magical halls? Hogwarts would certainly fall into a state of utter chaos if I were to abandon my post for even one day.

I must remain strong. For the students. For Hogwarts.

ROLLING TO VICTORY

It may seem simple, but *Accio* Ball is a game of skill that your opponents all take seriously. Stay calm, and get a sense of weight and momentum to win.

The Summoner's Court Elite

You receive an invite to continue your *Accio* Ball challenge against those rising stars of the Summoning Charm. When you're ready, return to the Summoner's Court outside Hogwarts.

Earlier on, Leander Prewett was happy to accept a draw as a sign of capability. Your next challenger, Samantha Dale, only settles for a win if you want to progress.

Samantha has arranged vortexes at four spots on the court, edging slow-moving balls out of play. This is a test of control and accuracy, getting momentum just right.

Three more challengers await after putting Samantha in her place, the rules of each round becoming more complex than the last. Successive rivals are savvier and more unforgiving.

The High Keep

Natty Onai has tracked Rookwood's thugs to Falbarton Castle, where she hopes to retrieve an incriminating letter. The only way in is to climb the battlements.

This quest tests puzzle-solving. First, cast *Depulso* on a storage room door mechanism to retrieve the box inside. Use this box to climb up and into the building.

After blasting away a wooden barricade, move the obstacle using *Accio* from a gap in the wall opposite. This same block can be used to find a treasure chest in the gate room where Natty eventually joins you. To raise the gate, use *Depulso*. Then quickly use *Accio* to lock it.

Before Natty can enter the front door, she is stopped in her tracks by Theophilus Harlow and his men. They have Highwing with them! As soon as they are gone, Natty sneaks in.

You progress by climbing the north wall and knocking a block down through a hole in the floor. As you make your way up the tower, you can deal with the trackers and stalkers using stealth. When you reach a locked door, you can shove the poachers over the walls by casting *Depulso*.

There's one last barricade to destroy on the south wall before climbing the last flight of steps to the top of the tower. Here you find two Hippogriffs that carry both you and Natty to safety.

As for that letter? Natty summoned it right out of Harlow's hands.

FLIGHT OF THE HIPPOGRIFFS

Your escape from Falbarton Castle is a spectacular sequence that elicits shouts of joy from Natty. The Hippogriff is a powerful and versatile mount.

Venomous Revenge

The "Venomous Revenge" Side Quest offers Mandrakes, Chomping Cabbages, Mallowsweet, and Dittany as finders-keepers rewards.

Ackley Barnes, found muttering behind the Three Broomsticks, urges you to grab his Venomous Tentacula plant from the cellar of his crafty business partner, Alfred Lawley.

The cellar door is opposite Zonko's Joke Shop. Once inside, Ackley is soon spotted pottering about. Your budding stealth tactics are put to the test. *Alohomora* opens an old door to the storage room, which is overrun by Thornback scurriours. There's no cheating your way out of the cellar via Floo Flames. Retrace your steps to claim a fistful of silver from Ackley for your efforts.

IT'S NEVER THAT EASY

If there is something valuable at stake, you can be sure that it is well guarded. Spiders are a widespread adversary and they always put up a fight.

The Hall of Herodiana

◆

Third-year student Sophronia Franklin cannot wait until her fifth year to learn *Depulso*. She wants you to solve a series of push-and-pull puzzles in her place. In return, you'll claim the attire of the famed Herodiana Byrne, "the greatest *Depulso* Master of all time."

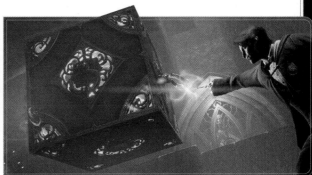

Sophronia, reached via the Charms Classroom Floo Flames, sends you to the foot of the Defense Against the Dark Arts tower. Here, casting *Depulso* shoves a large stone button, opening a door to Herodiana's masterpiece conundrum. It is a collection of huge blocks, some with handles for mobility. Position these to clamber out of each room and on to the next.

If at any point all seems lost, look for the gleaming spinning blocks that reset the larger blocks. A quick blast from any direction puts you back to square one. However, only the blocks revert to starting positions. You remain in place . . . a clue on how to solve Room Three.

The Tale of Rowland Oakes

The search for Adelaide Oakes's missing uncle is a tough, although thrilling, quest.

Rowland Oakes's last known location is north of Brocburrow. Poachers loiter in the approach to his campsite and can be avoided. Ranrok's Loyalists are guarding the place, however, and you need exceptional stealth tactics to outwit them. More likely this will be a fight, in which explosive barrels help to scatter the crowd.

Hello, please forgive the sudden request, but might I speak with you? I've not heard from my Uncle Rowland in quite some time. I've been beside myself with worry. Could you meet me in the courtyard?

Adelaide Oakes

There's no sign of Rowland, but a detailed journal is left behind with a map revealing his potential whereabouts: Korrow Ruins. Sketched landmarks point the way along the river.

ENTERING THE ARENA

When scouting larger strongholds, you'll often have time to assess battlegrounds before stirring up trouble. Stay out of sight and formulate a plan.

The ruins are accessed via an upper floor. Once inside, take a moment to plunder a chamber behind a statue. Light the brazier to rotate the plinth, and step on the button to spin again.

As you head south into the goblin lair, Loyalist rangers use crossbows to protect warriors and assassins. There is a huge locked door on the far wall, powered by a nearby steam-operated engine. Rowland is holed up in his cell in the west wing.

He needs his wand to escape the enchanted lock on the cell door, leaving you no choice but to risk what lies beyond that locked door. This is a cathedral, once splendid, now ransacked.

Take as many Loyalists by stealth as possible before alerting the named enemy Pergit. Or sneak quietly into the small anteroom, snatch the wand, and scramble away unnoticed.

Hand Rowland his wand and hear his story.

In the Shadow of the Estate

In this Relationship Quest, Sebastian Sallow introduces you to his ailing twin sister, Anne. He is desperate to find a cure, stopping at nothing. His uncle Solomon knows that there are limits.

As I mentioned, my sister Anne misses Hogwarts and she hasn't been herself lately. I'd like to take you up on your promise to visit her with me.

I'm heading to Feldcroft soon, so I'll look forward to seeing you there. It's just south of Hogwarts.

By the way, hope you're faring well with the Blasting Curse. It's still one of my favorites.

Sebastian

The Sallow family home is in Feldcroft, two thousand steps southwest of Hogwarts. You get caught in the middle of Seb's disagreements with his uncle Solomon, forced to intervene. How you respond to Solomon's doubts affects your relationship with Sebastian, so consider options with care. In the end, you are only deciding what is best for Anne and those around her who love her.

Sebastian is going after Ranrok's Loyalists who injured Anne while ransacking a nearby house. While searching the ruins, you find a fire-damaged painting of a woman, her face obscured. You recognize this place from the memory in the first Pensieve—the scene of the drought.

After more exploration, you blast through rubble to access a cellar, which has a crystallized stone portal linked to the Undercroft. Upon passing through, a triptych is revealed on the wall. Its left-hand panel painting shows the Overlook, which Seb recognizes. The triptych also hides a map that bears a rune symbol. It is proof that Ranrok is searching for something connected to the Keepers, and raises the possibility that Anne has been cursed by ancient magic.

Take the Biscuit

A goblin named Garnuff has a heartfelt plea to make in Hogsmeade. His beloved Biscuit, a Mooncalf, has been snatched by poachers. You swiftly agree to rescue his furry companion.

Biscuit is imprisoned far from Hogsmeade, in the region of East North Ford Bog. Get as close as you can using Floo Flames, and fly the rest of the way, silently by broom. Descend as soon as you catch sight of trouble to alight undetected. You have a far easier time this way.

Only a handful of poachers are milling about the campsite, and they are tidily taken care of using the Disillusionment Charm and *Petrificus Totalus* (and maybe a few distractions). Cast

Alohomora to bust out the skittish Mooncalves, one of which is Biscuit. The Slowing Charm, **ARRESTO MOMENTUM**, and Levitation Spell, *Levioso*, hold her gently in place while handling your nab-sack. Now, to make Garnuff's day.

Astronomy Class

Astronomy Class is taught rather strictly by Professor Shah. The class gathers on the observation deck of the Astronomy Tower, where you are partnered with a new friend, Amit Thakkar. Amit is a self-professed astronomy buff.

After learning how to focus the school telescope, Amit gifts you his older, but still excellent, model made with goblin-cut glass and inscribed with Gobbledegook (which Amit can read).

Amit invites you to join his hunt for astronomy tables around Hogwarts that point to hidden constellations. The first is somewhere along the old ramparts bordering the Quidditch pitch, beyond a series of rooms that require casting the Blasting Curse, *Confringo*, and the Fire-making Spell, *Incendio*, to clear boxes and cobwebs.

This particular astronomy table points to Lupus, the wolf. Here, and in all further examples, the simplest method is to keep the view central while making slight adjustments to zoom.

SATYAVATI SHAH

Astronomy Professor

After being raised largely in the Muggle world, Satyavati Shah took an interest in the sciences, which she carried with her into her schooling at Hogwarts. Afterward, she eventually took up a position as professor of Astronomy at Hogwarts. Shah devotes herself to her subject in a way that most would find extreme. Just like her scientific subject, she comes off to her pupils as cold, rigid, and demanding. She is easily carried away when talking about the heavens. Aloof and intimidating, Shah views many of the other Hogwarts disciplines (like Divination) as wishy-washy.

Rescuing Rococo

Agnes Coffey's pet has gotten lost in Henrietta's Hideaway, a palatial underground network of puzzles. Return Rococo safely, hunting down treasures galore while you're there.

A river troll and notorious Ashwinder Dunstan Trinity are among the enemies you encounter upon reaching Henrietta's Hideaway. You may sneak past them toward the south door.

There are two floors in Henrietta's Hideaway that dismantle and reassemble when stepped on. The first, heading north down a corridor, simply drops you in a dungeon to figure your way out. The second is more complicated because you need to cast **WINGARDIUM LEVIOSA** to trigger it before crossing. Float a nearby brazier to foil the trap or lure the scout in the room ahead.

Use the blocks marked with *Levioso* and *Confringo* symbols to activate platforms on either side of the north-side door in the final room. Rococo is playing in the room beyond. Raid the chest and return Rococo to Agnes.

A Thief in the Night

An Irondale man jumps to terrible conclusions about his sister, convinced that she has stolen a family heirloom. This doesn't seem to add up, but you agree to investigate.

Follow the trail of coins west a fair distance from the hamlet. It leads to a small campsite, where a (presumably) innocent Niffler is tending to its stash. You can nab-sack the Niffler before returning the heirloom (if you can find it) to Pádraic Haggarty, clearing his sister Catrin's name.

TREKKING BY TIME OF DAY

Some quests can only be fulfilled between certain hours, often enhancing the atmosphere. Should they occur at night, navigation is also trickier.

The Unique Unicorn

Betty Bugbrooke is found fretting in Hogsmeade's village circle. Betty has known Hazel the unicorn since she was a golden foal. Last time they met, Hazel got hurt saving Betty's life.

The nervous creature is in a den north of the village. Unlike Biscuit the Mooncalf, Hazel roams free. But, just like the Mooncalf, the Slowing Charm, *Arresto Momentum*, is needed to rescue her. Even under the cover of a Disillusionment Charm, Hazel senses your presence.

You may be surprised to find that Betty has no place to keep Hazel safe from harm, but she welcomes your offer to take good care of this beautiful creature at your private vivarium.

RESPECT
ALL WILDLIFE
How you behave around
magical beasts can help or
hinder your chances of
interacting with them.
Unicorns, for instance,
are easily startled.

The Second Trial: Charles Rookwood

Ranrok's Loyalists have taken Rookwood Castle, and you hurry there to meet Professor Fig.

You may challenge goblins head-on, or attempt sneakier options, before lining up a wooden block, casting *Wingardium Leviosa*, and climbing into the courtyard through the crumbled wall.

Ranrok's Loyalists and Ashwinders rally to capture you, under Ranrok's orders to Rookwood ("Bring me the child!"). You get a preview of what Ashwinder executioners are capable of and also how best to stop them: *Arresto Momentum* and *Expelliarmus*. Once inside the keep, a timed-switch puzzle opens the cellar door. Blast a screen on the wall to reveal a switch there.

Charles Rookwood says that you alone can take the trial and connect with ancient magic. The first reservoir activates a portal through which a tall pillar becomes a block to clamber on. The south exit is reached after passing through the portal once more.

Indeed, the theme of this trial is the use of portals to manipulate blocks. The second puzzle introduces you to the skill of gliding blocks through portals using *Wingardium Leviosa*. There is also a wall switch to spin the portal, to observe differences of appearance on either side.

When faced with Pensieve Protectors and Sentries, *Expelliarmus* works especially well against them. Before your next encounter, a crossroads contains a secret chest in the form of a block, which is transformed via the portal. Target the switch from the west platform.

Pensieve Protectors in the next room are only visible, and take damage, when viewed from one side of the portal. This switch-portal routine puts you in good stead for the final battle.

Before that, however, you realize that it is only after passing a block through the portal that it can function as a pillar once the walkway is aligned. Target the switch from the walkway one last time to face the east exit. Another room with a portal chest is in the next corridor.

Ranrok suspects there is more of it in Feldcroft. Do not return until you've found it.

What is Ranrok looking for? Maybe the rare metal Rowland Oakes mentioned?

In the final room, before the Pensieve Guardian appears, there are more Protectors and Sentries to face. Remember the portal trick here, but you'll have to be faster on your feet.

The Guardian succumbs briefly to *Arresto Momentum* and *Glacius*, but your main concern is his flail, blocked with *Protego* and responding with *Stupefy*. Keep basic casts flying, putting the Guardian under pressure. It eventually falls, severely weakened by ancient magic finishers.

The Lost Child

Natty Onai is hot on Rookwood and Harlow's trail, leading her to a grieving widow whose son is also now missing. You arrange to meet at Johanna Bickle's home in Lower Hogsfield.

Archie Bickle is only a young boy and may have witnessed his father's murder at the hands of Harlow. You waste no time in your attempt to track him down at his most likely location, a hideout south of the hamlet. Early signs are not good—a wolf pack pacing the abandoned campsite. However, casting *Revelio* shows Archie's footprints heading west into the wilds.

   Your sense of unease increases at the sight of Thestrals, which both you and Natty can see. As you advance through the forest, a fork in the road calls for *Revelio* to confirm direction, showing multiple sets of footprints. Proof, hard to admit, that Archie has been captured.

You engage with Ashwinders at their camp where Archie is being held. Upon entering a tent, more determined enemies guard their prize, among them notorious villain Catrin Haggarty. When the dust settles, you find Archie locked in a cage and return him safely to his mother.

⬥⬥⬥ THESTRALS ⬥⬥⬥

Thestrals are strange creatures with a bad reputation. They resemble winged horses in size, shape, and wingspan, but there the similarities end. They have skeletal bodies, reptilian features, bat-like, leathery wings, and love the taste of blood. They are considered dark omens, bringing misfortune down on any who encounter them, as only those who have witnessed death are able to see them. However, these creatures are highly intelligent herd animals who are able to understand riders' commands and are fiercely loyal to their friends and owners.

In the Shadow of the Bloodline and In the Shadow of the Study

Sebastian and Ominis have drastically opposing views on the use of Dark Arts. To progress your quest, the boys need to find common ground.

First, convince Ominis to access the Scriptorium of Salazar Slytherin. Have him reveal the whereabouts of the Scriptorium without betraying your own morals. Eventually he helps.

Access to the Scriptorium then requires lighting three braziers in order. Casting *Revelio* and a keen eye for nearby detail shows how it's done. A doorway slides open in the wall behind Ominis.

The chambers beyond are littered with letters from Ominis's aunt, Noctua Gaunt. You cast *Reparo* to reassemble a wall-mounted stone relief. The hissing sound is Parseltongue, which Ominis understands because he is a Parselmouth. He uses this ability to open the next door.

I must prove my point— we do not need to use the Dark Arts as my family instructs. When I reach the Scriptorium, I will find evidence that there's more to Salazar Slytherin than we realize.

I have written to my brother. He now knows how I accessed the corridor's entrance and that there's no straight path to reach the Scriptorium. It's a maze with many challenges to solve.

I hope that my brother will follow my lead and we can study our ancestor's legacy together.

Noctua Gaunt

I've lost hope. I'm locked in.
I heard a scream and saw the tortured
faces. The only way forward is with an
Unforgivable Curse. Even if I wanted
to cast it, I have no one upon whom
to do so. Salazar Slytherin created
a malicious challenge indeed.

In my last correspondence to my
brother, I'd invited him here. Now, if
he looks for me alone, I'll have led
him to his death. Despite our
differences, I wish him no ill. I wish
we had parted on better terms.

Noctua Gaunt

To unlock all further doors, you must match symbols etched into them—some worn and obscured—to icons on switches close by. Beside these switches are braziers, which, once lit, begin a short countdown. Fail to lock in the combination, and the guardian snake strikes.

Eventually you reach a frightful door that needs the Unforgivable Curse **CRUCIO** to unlock. You may learn *Crucio* from Sebastian, choosing to turn it on him or to suffer its effects. In any case, you must proceed. Consider your actions wisely because they are irreversible.

The Scriptorium is every bit as enchanting yet sinister as you can imagine. You collect Salazar Slytherin's spellbook, gather treasure, then leave via the statue at the back of the room.

SMALL TASKS, BIG PROBLEMS

Be prepared to go to great lengths in order to claim the lowliest quest items, and always be on your guard. Mighty enemies never waste an opportunity.

Spot Removal

A Hufflepuff student has found a cure for acne. The recipe requires the pus from a bubotuber, so on behalf of Sacharissa Tugwood, you set out once more for the Forbidden Forest.

Far from inviting some peaceful handpicking, the area is home to a high-level forest troll. His routine is familiar, but shoulder barges, club swipes, and thrown boulders hit hard.

Once defeated, a couple bubotubers are found in the troll's lair. Three more are along the forest trail, where Dark Mongrels are on patrol. As soon as you have five, Sacharissa has all that she needs to help her dermatologically disadvantaged peers.

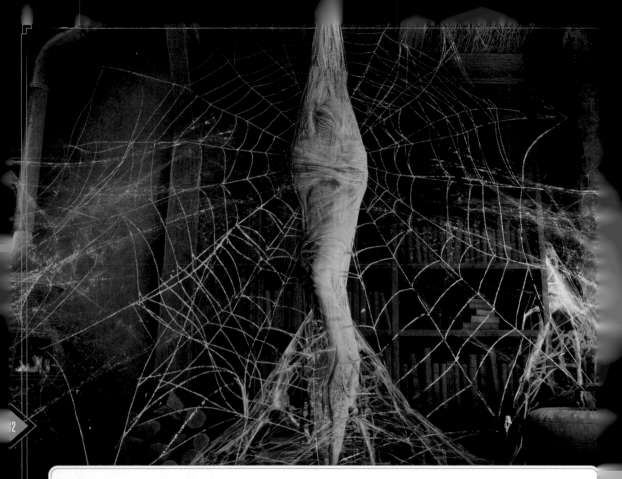

Tangled Web

Crispin Dunne's Aranshire hamlet is crawling with Thornbacks. Last he knew, his friend Mary Portman was trapped inside her cottage. A straightforward rescue mission? Not exactly . . .

You clear the hamlet and find Mary cocooned in her living room. That is only the start of the horror. Beneath Mary's home is a cellar, where this entrepreneurial lady was managing her ambitious silk business. The cellar sits above a huge cave and Thornback breeding ground. The place is writhing with egg sacs ready to burst any moment. Yes, all must be destroyed.

You may find yourself bound by silk, targeted by scurriours and ambushers. Do not struggle! Wait for the command to free yourself: Keep your calm, especially when a matriarch and the Insatiable Spider enter the chamber.

Casting *Incendio, Confringo, Glacius,* and *Arresto Momentum* serves you well. Show no fear!

CALMNESS IN THE STORM

The "Tangled Web" Side Quest gives you a taste for frantic combat, with spiders attacking from all sides. It helps to keep track of fast-moving targets.

Fire and Vice

Poppy is waiting for you north of Hogwarts, hot on the trail of Rookwood's poachers.

Your destination is Horntail Hall, the poachers' "best-kept secret," where Poppy hopes to learn more of their plans. As you travel through the forest, the Centaurs accuse you of being in league with the poachers but are dissuaded otherwise. You continue the search for signs of poacher activity, finding goblin swords and armor at one camp—all highly suspicious.

Following the trail south leads to a tent that appears modest on the outside, but inside is revealed to be Horntail Hall. It's a dragon fighting ring! No wonder Centaurs dislike wizardkind.

Stealthily circle the south side of the ring, beneath the stands. You discover a large room where a dragon is being held captive, and in one alcove is a Hebridean dragon egg.

It is possible to use a stealth attack on all but two of the initial enemies, leaving only the guards on overwatch. However, an Animagus Apparates in to finish the fight, accompanied by rangers and trackers. Rather than take them on, you cast *Accio* on the dragon's shackle, freeing the beast to turn on its tormentors. It doesn't go well for them; one executioner is even eaten!

THE HEBRIDEAN BLACK EGG

The Hebridean Black is a dragon species native to the Hebridean islands of Scotland. It has brilliant purple eyes and lays purple eggs. Its favorite food is deer.

"Beeting" a Curse

An anxious Samantha Dale is looking worried by the Greenhouse. The Ravenclaw student's kid brother William has succumbed to a family curse, his feet Transfigured into purple beets.

To cure William, all you need to do is return the Dale family crest to the resting place of Marmaduke Dale. This ought to undo the mischief caused by this ancestor's besmirched, jealous older sibling—Samantha has all the details.

It's a short journey to the tomb by broom, flying east out of Brocburrow.

SHIELDING TO SURVIVE
The Shield Charm, *Protego*, becomes a mainstay of your combat repertoire the farther you tread into the adventure. Master its timing to survive.

mightier than any river or forest troll, hurling rocks and swiping at close range with his club. Time your Shielding Spell to absorb the impact.

Place the crest in Marmaduke's sarcophagus in the chamber beyond, then head back to Samantha, who has received word from St. Mungo's that William's feet are back to normal.

In the Shadow of the Mine

Since our visit to Feldcroft, something's dawned on me about the triptych we found. Meet me at the Overlook, just north of the Forbidden Forest, and I'll explain.

Sebastian

Overlook Mine is guarded by goblins. You can (try to) avoid detection or deal blows. If you do intend to slink past, take the route behind the watchtower.

Rail tracks lead the way to the next sign of trouble—more of Ranrok's Loyalists. Hugging the southeast side of the mountain takes you through a tunnel, leading directly to the mine.

Spiderwebs hang everywhere. The Fire-making Spell, *Incendio*, sears them before you slide into the next room, clattering into goblins. Use the Levitation Charm, *Wingardium Leviosa,* to move a box and climb your way out.

In the chamber where water drips from the opening high above, the Mending Charm, *Reparo*, grants passage across the broken bridge. The Fire-making Spell, *Incendio*, reveals more chests and goblin stashes. When venomous scurriours strike, be prepared for the command that will help you break free of thread.

Overlook Mine sets the example for ignoring waypoint markers to discover lost treasures. Remember that *Lumos* pushes back Devil's Snare, as do braziers ignited with *Confringo*.

Things get heated when Loyalist warriors, rangers, and their commander are joined by venomous scurriours and matriarchs. Casting *Protego* with *Stupefy* will help you stay in the fight. Disable and disarm using *Arresto Momentum*, *Glacius*, and *Expelliarmus*.

When all this is over, use *Confringo* from a distance to melt away the web obscuring the switch on the northwest wall. Casting *Incendio* exposes the switch by the door on ground level, which is the last to activate using three basic casts in rapid succession. Clear more webs to enter.

Isidora Morganach's hideaway is a "cavern within a cavern." After finding the second canvas piece here, you exit through the southeast wall to the Undercroft.

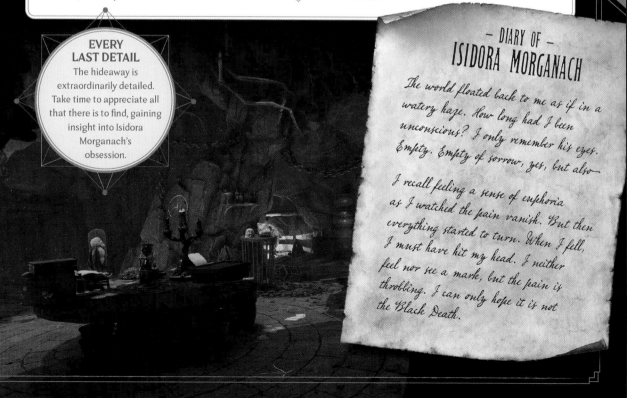

EVERY LAST DETAIL
The hideaway is extraordinarily detailed. Take time to appreciate all that there is to find, gaining insight into Isidora Morganach's obsession.

— DIARY OF —
ISIDORA MORGANACH

The world floated back to me as if in a watery haze. How long had I been unconscious? I only remember his eyes. Empty. Empty of sorrow, yes, but also—

I recall feeling a sense of euphoria as I watched the pain vanish. But then everything started to turn. When I fell, I must have hit my head. I neither feel nor see a mark, but the pain is throbbing. I can only hope it is not the Black Death.

In the Shadow of Time

You meet Sebastian at the Feldcroft Catacomb, to search for a relic that might save his sister's life. Inside there are student reports scattered around, like the ones slotted into Salazar Slytherin's spellbook. They contain clues on how to solve the conundrums ahead.

The catacomb is a complex location that rewards exploration. In the first room, guarded by spiders, you can use a box to climb and reach a chest. In the second room, casting *Accio* busts open a door on the west wall leading to more chests. But beware of spiders every step of the way.

Your main concern is the circular Great Hall, and a sarcophagus at its center covered in human bones. Using *Wingardium Leviosa*, float them to form an archway around the locked door in order to progress. More bones are tidied away in drawers, opened with *Accio*. Still more are beyond the southeast door, which can be blasted through. Sneaking beneath the collapsed section on the north side of the hall leads to a passageway, more bones (if you need them), and a treasure chest that you may have spotted behind bars.

Sebastian offers to teach **IMPERIO**, the Imperius Curse, to control the minds of enemies. It is the second of three Unforgivable Curses to accept or decline. This choice is yours to make.

The south door is your main exit route, but you may also wish to explore east and west for more treasure, using force to gain entry. And, yes, there are serious spiders, so be prepared. To continue your mission, use *Accio* to pull handles that match both symbols on the panels.

The Relic Room involves a lengthy battle against spiders, including matriarchs. Survive this and burn through the webbing that covers the entire east wall. Here you find a final note, advising, "Until we know more, please do not remove this relic," which Sebastian ignores.

I foolishly mentioned the relic in my report and was reminded to leave it where it lay. But research must come before my fealty to the rules. I sense something about this relic.

I was told that those chosen by English Oak wands have powerful intuition. I believe it.

Therefore, when no one was looking, I acted. I conjured two barricades to isolate the relic. Ancestors forgive me, but I used their very bones as the key.

I plan to return to it, but first I must ready myself for our next assignment: learning the Imperius Curse. The spell is said to serve well against enemies.

You may try to advise him against it, but Seb claims the relic no matter what. It requires a Dark Sacrifice to realize its potential. Ominis, who followed you here, worries for his friend.

Feldcroft is under attack from Ranrok's Loyalists when you return. A goblin assassin almost takes Anne's life, but she is saved when Sebastian cries *Imperio*. Well, it certainly has its uses.

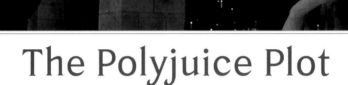

The Polyjuice Plot

The third trial begins in the headmaster's office, but only Professor Black and his house-elf Scrope know the entry password. You must disguise yourself as Black and trick Scrope into telling.

First, you need Polyjuice Potion, which transfigures a person into the exact appearance of someone else. Thankfully, Professor Fig has a vial prepared and urges you to drink.

Being Professor Black involves berating students and belittling professors wherever you find them. At Hogwarts this means almost everywhere, and you must never give the game away. It also allows you to glean embarrassing personal details, as long as you keep a straight face.

Madam Kogawa knows of Scrope's movements. She is on the bridge connecting the Library Annex with the Viaduct Courtyard. Critical of Black's cancellation of Quidditch for the season, the nonplussed professor points you to the Great Hall. Professor Weasley is the penultimate hurdle, engaging in awkward conversation. At last, you must persuade the unfailingly loyal Scrope as best you can to give up the information, gaining you entry into the headmaster's office.

POLYJUICE POTION

Polyjuice is a potion that allows the drinker to assume the form of someone else. It's not an easy potion to brew, nor transformation to undertake, but it can allow the drinker to infiltrate and trick almost anyone. The potion is so complex, it takes a month to brew properly and requires a piece of the person you wish to turn into, such as a few strands of hair.

All's Well That Ends Bell

Rumor has it that the headmaster has an aversion to the sound of school bells, since they remind him of his wedding day. True or not, Black called for them to be dismantled.

Evangeline Bardsley thinks this is the ideal opportunity to irritate Professor Black, and on an hourly basis. She asks that you replace the missing bells so that they may ring, loudly, again.

Evangeline directs you to the Music Room, which sits below the Bell Tower. This takes you to the Entrance Wing of Hogwarts, up many flights of stairs, and yet more stairs from the Music Room to the tower. Use *Revelio* to spot various helpful chests while you're there.

The bells are hoisted into place using *Wingardium Leviosa*, arranging them in order of size. When you're done, to escape the commotion of pealing bells, go outside onto the balcony. A gilded chest and ornate box are yours to find. Few students would think to come here.

A Basis for Blackmail

Natty Onai asks you to dig up more dirt on Rookwood and Harlow in Hogsmeade. While Natty keeps a low profile, you quiz locals on their latest crimes.

Agabus Philbert, Daisy Rabe, and Otto Dibble have gripes to share. You go to inform Natty, but she is missing. Natty's footprints lead to her wand, dropped deliberately behind the Hog's Head. This clue leads you to the cellar door and a secret Ashwinder hideout.

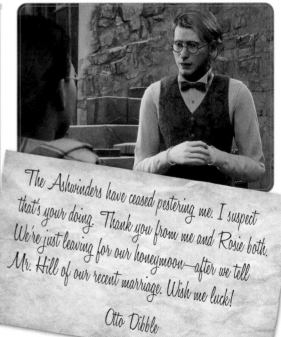

The Ashwinders have ceased pestering me. I suspect that's your doing. Thank you from me and Rosie both. We're just leaving for our honeymoon—after we tell Mr. Hill of our recent marriage. Wish me luck!

Otto Dibble

Use *Accio* to open the fake beer-barrel entrance. Inside, the scene comprises an assassin, executioner, and Ashwinder leader Gwendolyn Zhou. Stay unseen and take the left corridor, casting *Petrificus Totalus* on all you meet. The trick is to avoid Gwendolyn's hawklike gaze.

Your silent circuit takes you beneath the wooden stairs to a grate. A solitary scout stands in the way of Natty in the holding cells. Here, you also meet

Isko Rabe, whose wand is needed to break both he and Natty free. Casting *Revelio* points to a box on the table, and Isko's wand is inside.

It is left for you and Natty to escape, past Ashwinders that escaped petrification earlier. With echoes of combative magic still in the air, collect Agabus's book of poems from the box on the bar, and Otto's love letter above a flight of wooden stairs in the southeast corner.

PART 4:
WANDS AT THE READY

In the Shadow of the Mountain

Your combat smarts are stretched in this mission to secure the final triptych canvas. In the approach to the tower tunnel, goblins guard drill machines on the switchbacks. Get in the habit of casting *Revelio*, exposing hillside doorways and a Thestral nest off the beaten track.

Sebastian initiates the fight against a goblin camp, where your shield counters are essential. Keep your eyes peeled for lucrative areas—a cave to the west, especially, hiding an ornate chest.

Ranrok's Loyalist warriors and an assassin guard the tunnel entrance. Once past them, you face a frantic Thornback assault. Keep scanning for detours, including one before starting your descent.

Following another extended clash against all Thornback archetypes, expose any webbed-up switches with the Blasting Curse, *Confringo*. Target the switch to the left-side door last of all.

Ahead, you will face a mountain troll. During this encounter it is better to quash its arachnid accomplices while dodging the heavy attacks. Just one shoulder barge can deplete most of your stamina. In time, your efforts will wear him down. To progress further, repair all the damage done.

Notes from Isidora Morganach confirm you are on the right track. Follow Sebastian to search for ways forward. To open the ancient magic gateway, clear away the rubble, then target the south-wall switch. Inside Isidora's last-known hiding place she has left a note to her rightful successor. Bag the canvas and leave.

STAY ON YOUR FEET

You have only slim second chances when up against the mountain troll. Sebastian helps by keeping at least some of the spiders busy while you brawl.

Flight Tests

If you have a love of flying, do not miss any chance to push broom performance. After proving yourself as a gifted rider, an opportunity arises to explore the outer limits.

Quidditch may be canceled, but Slytherin captain Imelda Reyes has reopened trial courses that test speed, stamina, and spatial awareness. You hear of this via Albie Weekes at Spintwiches, who asks you to research a series of broom upgrades.

Trial number one is at the Quidditch pitch next to Hogwarts. This gets you in the habit of visualizing height and speed ahead of the turns. Imelda concludes that "you're not terrible."

Your report to Albie notes that the basic broom is turbulent and wants for speed at altitude; you also find it drifts to the left. In exchange for the info, and 2 Gold, Albie presents Upgrade I.

This first upgrade increases acceleration and speed, adding one stamina bar. It shaves five seconds off your Quidditch pitch performance. But let's see how this fares at Irondale.

The second of Imelda's trials is a scenic flight from

REMEMBER TO BLINK

With each new upgrade, the handling of the broom feels tighter and more responsive. Your focus begins shifting rapidly from hoop to hoop as you fly.

Hogsmeade. Through steep ascents, descents, and sharp turns, you hand in what Imelda says is "a bloody good run." You report that performance is a tad shaky at top speed, with handling wobbly in strong gusts of wind. This, Albie aims to address with Upgrade II, for which you take another financial hit.

You speed to the South Coast Course, spooking Ashwinders and Ranrok's lot where your route flies over them. The Clagmar Coast is accessed via Coastal Cavern in Hogwarts Valley. Your reward for beating Imelda's time there is the Moon Trimmer broom, which is *quick*.

Upgrade II is, for sure, the best upgrade yet—incredibly nimble, though the wind catches beneath the seat a bit, owing to the speeds it reaches. Albie needs longer than usual to craft Upgrade III, his final effort. Be grateful for the time it takes to save the 25 Gold that Albie charges.

You may be left penniless, but Albie's masterwork is perfection.

History of Magic Class

Professor Binns's lesson in History of Magic sends all his students, you included, to sleep. You catch something about a 1752 goblin rebellion and its effects on the wizard milling industry, awaking just in time to join Binns's tour of historical displays.

Absent-minded Binns meanders through the names of significant members of wizardkind and goblins, including politician Eargit the Ugly and artisan Bragbor the Boastful, whose name you recall. Indeed, Bragbor was an ancestor of Ranrok. He earned renown for exquisite goblin metallurgy, commissioned by the Keepers.

You receive instruction to find Field Guide pages on Grimbald Weft, Sir Affpuddle the waving knight, and a plaque in remembrance of the Belltower Plague. Your *Revelio* skills may have missed one or all of these. In any case, Binns's Ranrok background info is useful.

PROFESSOR CUTHBERT BINNS

History of Magic Professor

Although not much is known about his early life, Professor Binns had been teaching at Hogwarts for decades before he died, and decades after. He is the only professor at Hogwarts who also happens to be a ghost. Some say he is unaware that he's dead but he does tend to float through the blackboard at the end of a lesson. At his oldest age in life, he went down to the staffroom and fell asleep in a chair in front of the fire. But he died in his sleep and simply got up to go to his next lecture as a ghost.

Portrait in a Pickle

You need at least *Alohomora* Level 2 to complete this quest on behalf of a musty old portrait. This entails gathering nine Demiguise statues for Gladwin Moon. Once you have these, speak with the painting of Ferdinand Octavius Pratt, which hangs in the Hogwarts Library. Pratt claims his other frame has been kidnapped.

You discover a fourth-year student, Astoria Crickett, paid thieves to "relocate" Pratt from his hook in the Three Broomsticks. He'd been snitching on students for Professor Black, making preposterous claims against them. Pratt believes his other frame may be somewhere near the coastline.

On an island linked to the mainland by a long, stone footpath are the Marunweem Ruins. Pratt is held beneath the ruins with a swarm of moths. Let Pratt know who's boss before returning his portrait to the Three Broomsticks.

FERDINAND OCTAVIUS PRATT

Ferdinand Octavius Pratt is possibly the most irritating and offensive portrait currently hanging in Hogwarts Library and the Three Broomsticks. Pratt is a selfish, conceited, and flamboyant character who spends his time fishing for compliments about his lavish appearance or pretending to be asleep so he can eavesdrop on students. He is a terrible gossip and uses secrets as leverage against students and teachers alike. Be careful what you say around him.

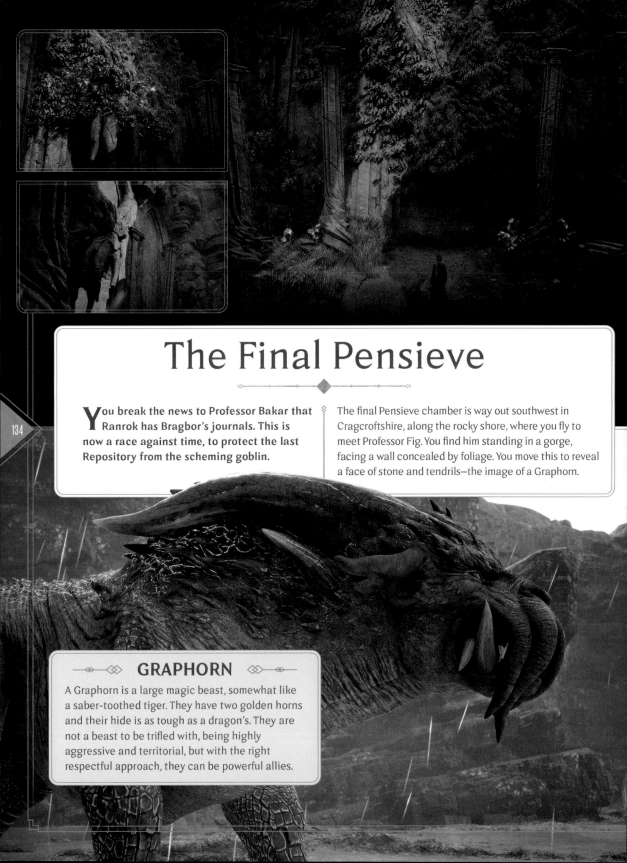

The Final Pensieve

You break the news to Professor Bakar that Ranrok has Bragbor's journals. This is now a race against time, to protect the last Repository from the scheming goblin.

The final Pensieve chamber is way out southwest in Cragcroftshire, along the rocky shore, where you fly to meet Professor Fig. You find him standing in a gorge, facing a wall concealed by foliage. You move this to reveal a face of stone and tendrils—the image of a Graphorn.

GRAPHORN

A Graphorn is a large magic beast, somewhat like a saber-toothed tiger. They have two golden horns and their hide is as tough as a dragon's. They are not a beast to be trifled with, being highly aggressive and territorial, but with the right respectful approach, they can be powerful allies.

An etching beneath your feet shows that this creature is needed to open the huge doors. Professor Fig knows that a Graphorn has its lair on the South Clagmar Coast. When you spy the remains of a large sea creature, Fig says, you're in the right place.

The ensuing duel is breathlessly fought, the Graphorn respectfully putting up one heck of a fight. The Freezing Spell, *Glacius*, is by far your most useful ally, but timing is everything. Wait for the creature to pounce, casting as its paws leave the ground. It is

folly to turn and run. In the moment that the Graphorn seems defeated, you consider whether to sustain your attack or kneel.

Having earned the Graphorn's trust, you ride back to where Professor Fig is waiting. Along the way, poachers are knocked off their feet by the creature's advancing bulk. Sure enough, when the Graphorn meets the stare of its stone-faced counterpart, the walls part.

RIDING THE GRAPHORN
The majestic Graphorn makes ground trips memorable. Feel proud that you gained the trust of such a creature.

THE INFERI
You face a mighty struggle against the undead in the catacomb, clawed closer to your own demise with each jagged-nailed swipe. It is a furious fight.

In the Shadow of the Relic

It's time to go back to Feldcroft Catacomb with Anne and Ominis, where Sebastian has ceased listening to reason. You battle legions of Inferi in pursuit of your troubled friend, weakening them with fire. Anne, concerned for her brother, goes to fetch Solomon, who might talk him out of this.

Anne's worried. She said Sebastian promised her that I would be there if she went to meet him in the catacomb. But now he's asking her to join him immediately and to come alone. She says he doesn't sound himself.

Meet us at the catacomb as soon as you can.

I hope that my quill has conveyed my message clearly.

Ominis

You discover that Sebastian is controlling the Inferi, which attacked you. In the connecting room, a staircase is built from bones as before. Sebastian is consumed by his mission, insisting that "the relic is the answer." Finally, Solomon arrives to intervene, summoning the relic to him before crushing the cursed artifact. You partner with Sebastian to subdue his uncle, but Sebastian takes things too far and casts **AVADA KEDAVRA**, killing Solomon instantly.

Anne witnesses the fall and she crumbles. Will you support or condemn Sebastian's actions?

A Bird in the Hand

◈————————◆————————◈

Poppy, with the aid of a Centaur, finds clues to the whereabouts of Golden Snidgets. You first need a Moonstone, which the Centaur believes is being held in a cave nearby.

Inside the cave you find a special Moonstone garden, guarded by a Cottongrass Dugbog. Before you reach the Moonstone, look for an ornate chest. The chest is hidden behind vines that you must incinerate. A moth-activated key summons a moving platform built of stone.

 Your route heads down to a room with moth spinners. Their keys are fluttering behind panels, activated by casting *Accio* on matching levers. After opening the door, the same moths are lured to the next room, raising a bridge and a pillar carrying another moth.

> *Are you familiar with the hamlet of Irondale? It's south of the castle.*
>
> *I think the cave where Dorran wants us to find the Moonstone may be located near there.*
>
>   *Poppy*

Two Great Spined Dugbogs guard the entrance to the Moonstone resting place, for which you must dive beneath bubbling waters. The Moonstone is taken to a henge, along a firefly trail. Once inserted into the henge, the Moonstone attracts Mooncalves that perform a sacred dance, leaving trails that glow in the grass. These form an important symbol.

You arrive at the ruin indicated by the Mooncalf dance. The Centaur Dorran is waiting, watching as you solve the puzzle to open a mysterious door.

Two conical pillars carry orbs representing the sun and moon, casting shadows on symbols arranged on the floor. The sun and moon shadows correspond with symbols on the door.

Your aim once inside is to release the towering wooden doors on the eastmost wall. Doing so involves floating elemental blocks onto matching podiums: fire and ice. The latter block is reached by stacking boxes and climbing up to a balcony near the entrance. The fire block is entangled in vines behind the podiums. Prime the two blocks using *Confringo* and *Glacius*.

Duelists, rangers, and stalkers Apparate into the room. Break their shields to defeat them. However, the fight continues as poachers Apparate into the

overgrown enclosure. Shield counters and casting *Protego* at the right time will keep the visitors busy until Dorran and a Centaur friend arrive. Trackers and Animagi are tricky, but with enemies focused on Dorran you can pick your targets.

One last gateway opens, which has protected Golden Snidget eggs for centuries. With the charm broken, the eggs hatch, and Dorran's Centaurs vow to guard them with their lives.

Crafting the Ancient Magic Wand

You claimed more than vital knowledge from the Keepers' Pensieves. Each one bestowed an artifact, until now of unknown purpose. You learn that they are components of a unique wand, which can be used only for one purpose: to access the Repository beneath Hogwarts.

You take these pieces to Gerbold Ollivander in Hogsmeade. Professor Fig sends an owl to advise the wandmaker of your imminent arrival. Gerbold admits to only ever conducting repairs in his workshop but welcomes the challenge. He vanishes into the back room while you pace the floor, staring out the window.

After you obtain the wand, you see Victor Rookwood lurking in the street. He goads you with insults, claiming the last Repository is his birthright. It becomes clear his taunts are a distraction as one of his henchmen appears behind you, grabbing you and Disapparating. This will be Rookwood's final mistake.

THE POWER TO END IT ALL

Though you may be uncertain of your own strength even now, there is no doubt that you have shown your worthiness. This is your fight to finish.

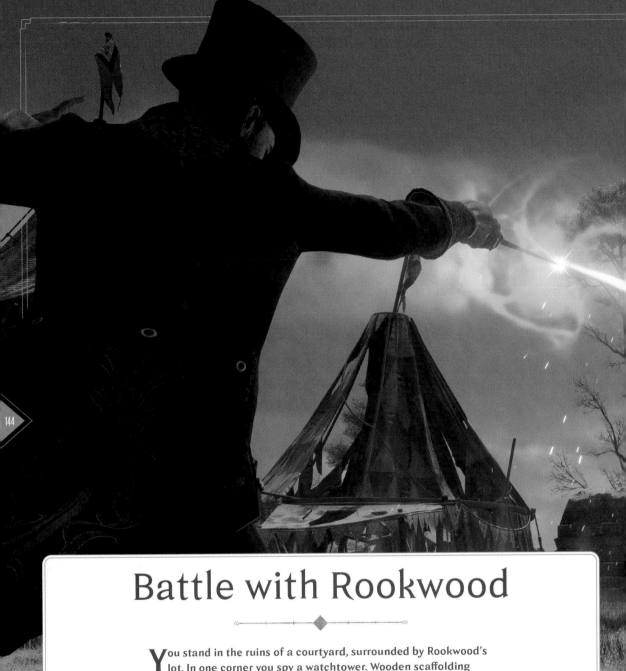

Battle with Rookwood

◆

You stand in the ruins of a courtyard, surrounded by Rookwood's lot. In one corner you spy a watchtower. Wooden scaffolding supports more ranged fighters along the adjacent wall.

Phase one of this encounter pits you against Ashwinder soldiers, scouts, and executioners. The latter you need to keep at bay, with *Expelliarmus* and *Arresto Momentum,* while picking off the other—comparatively weaker—foes. *Protego* and *Stupefy* counter lighter attacks. Be ready to break free of binding spells. Victor Rookwood steps in when his cronies wither. It requires an ancient magic finisher to remove Rookwood's shield, after which he sustains some damage.

More Ashwinder scouts and rangers Apparate into the arena, accompanied by an assassin. The ruckus has also attracted Inferi, who become priority targets as you dodge relatively harmless *Diffindo* blasts. Late-arriving Ashwinder scouts cast *Petrificus Totalus*, which causes serious damage. Search for Wiggenweld Potions on the perimeter to replenish supplies.

In the final phase, an Ashwinder duelist and poacher stalker enter the fray. You may have cause to unleash that ancient magic finisher on lesser foes, but as enemy ranks wear thin, it is best left to weaken Rookwood. As soon as his shield fails, hit him with everything you've got!

AN ENEMY MISJUDGED

Victor Rookwood is a show-off and a coward, sending in his underlings to weaken—or so he vainly hopes—his prized target. He underestimated you.

Harlow's Last Stand

Natty appreciates your support but cannot abandon her vengeful quest to see Harlow's and Rookwood's cronies brought down. You meet at Manor Cape, where Harlow was last seen.

There is no shying away from this fight as poachers and Ashwinders assemble. There are two waves of enemies that have you surrounded no matter where you take up position. Seek higher ground on the courtyard balcony for a notable advantage.

Please meet me near Manor Cape as soon as possible.
I received an interesting owl from Johanna Bickle about Harlow.

Natty

This battle involves near constant use of *Protego*, *Stupefy*, and shield breakage. It is enough to keep enemies suppressed while focusing on one target. Natty fights with conviction and has your back. When Harlow arrives to intimidate you, he is swiftly brought to his knees.

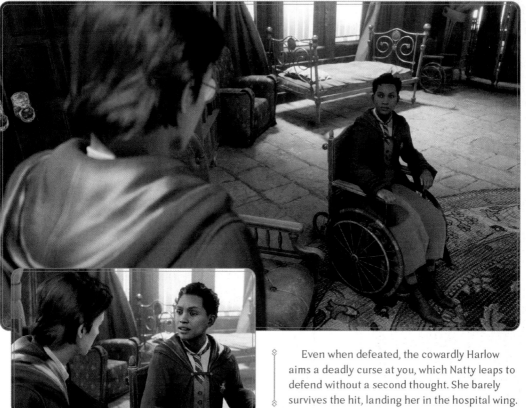

Even when defeated, the cowardly Harlow aims a deadly curse at you, which Natty leaps to defend without a second thought. She barely survives the hit, landing her in the hospital wing.

The Final Repository

After instructions are received from the Keepers in the Map Chamber, the floor melts
away to reveal the final Repository. Together with Professor Fig, you enter the Keepers'
caverns hidden beneath Hogwarts. Straightaway, a goblin drill machine crashes into view.

You race to claim the Repository, fighting high-ranking Loyalists, most protected by shields. Another drill penetrates the cavern, which Professor Fig uses his magic to throw aside.

DESIGNS ON DESTRUCTION

Goblin craftsmanship is remarkable, most of the time admirable, but under Ranrok's orders such artistry is misused. His drill machines are monstrous.

THE HARDER THEY FALL

Help from Professor Fig is gratefully received as you topple this towering, raging duo. Fig engages one troll while you duel against the other.

Two armored trolls occupy the next rocky arena, with fast-moving Loyalists in support. Tackle the smaller, weaker foes first. Take the trolls one at a time. Your ancient magic perception shows a way forward, where more Loyalists present a stiffer challenge.

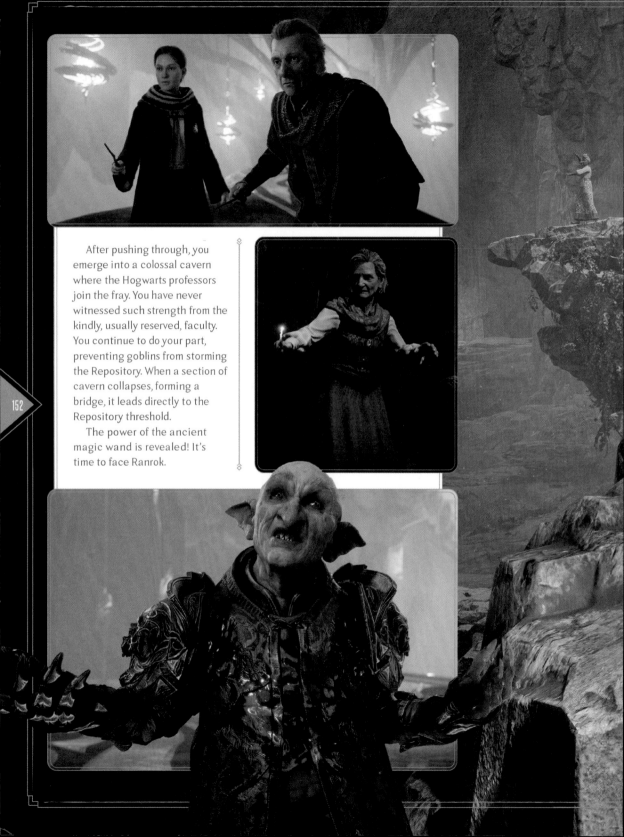

After pushing through, you emerge into a colossal cavern where the Hogwarts professors join the fray. You have never witnessed such strength from the kindly, usually reserved, faculty. You continue to do your part, preventing goblins from storming the Repository. When a section of cavern collapses, forming a bridge, it leads directly to the Repository threshold.

The power of the ancient magic wand is revealed! It's time to face Ranrok.

THE BEST OF HOGWARTS

Spells light up the cavern as the Hogwarts professors call upon their combined wisdom, laying their lives on the line to support your mission.

154

CUNNING TO THE END

Ranrok may be obsessed, but he is no fool, as the final battle proves. Your instinct may tell you to target the dragon, but that would be too obvious.

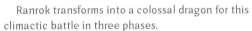

Ranrok transforms into a colossal dragon for this climactic battle in three phases.

In phase one, Ranrok hovers in the space above you, summoning orbs that you must target using spells of matching color. This exposes Ranrok to damage from your strongest attacks.

The number of orbs increases during phase two, in which you can also hurl the Red Binding projectiles back at Ranrok to stun him. The need to dodge and cast *Protego* increases.

During the final phase, Ranrok continues his strategy until his stamina falls below halfway. At this

point he lands to make his final bid to kill you. This includes breathing fire, sweeping across the cavern floor, distracting you from the business of smashing orbs and landing hits.

With Ranrok defeated, you face one last challenge. The final Repository remained buried beneath Hogwarts for good reason. Yet, in his wisdom, Professor Fig places the future of the artifact in your hands. As rightful protector, what shall be done with it? Make your choice . . .

Hogwarts Hero

After you vanquish Ranrok, the whole school rightly celebrates your incredible achievement. As a diligent student, however, you return to your Field Guide in search of anything you might've missed along the way. The world outside the Great Hall waits to greet you.

Now is the time to explore without pressure—rounding up the last of Ranrok's Loyalists and Rookwood's bewildered stragglers, completing Merlin Trials, and securing all lost treasures. Enjoy this freedom. You surely earned it.

REFERENCE LIBRARY

Infamous Foes

If you find your confidence raised after successive wins in battle, this would be a good time to hunt down some named enemies. There are more than twenty of these unique high-level targets to vanquish, in exchange for huge XP, high-value rewards, and another box ticked in the Field Guide Challenge.

PERGIT
Level 15–23 Loyalist Commander
Encountered: "The Tale of Rowland Oakes"

TEMPESTE THORNE
Level 15–25 Poacher Duelist
Encountered: In Highlands after "The High Keep"

THE INSATIABLE SPIDER
Level 16–25 Thornback Matriarch
Encountered: "Tangled Web"

BARDOLPH BEAUMONT'S CORPSE
Level 17–25 Inferius
Encountered: "Brother's Keeper"

RAMPANT DUGBOG
Level 17–25 Stoneback Dugbog
Encountered: Always available in Highlands

BELGRUFF THE BLUDGEONER
Level 20 Loyalist Commander
Encountered: "The Second Trial: Charles Rookwood"

ALEXANDRA'S TROLL
Level 20–30 Mountain Troll
Encountered: "Troll Control"

THE GRIM
Level 20–30 Dark Mongrel
Encountered: Always available in Highlands

OGBERT THE ODD
Level 20–30 Loyalist Sentinel
Encountered: Always available in Highlands

THE RIPARIAN TROLL

Level 20–30 River Troll

Encountered: "Descendant's Request"

THE WHITE WOLF

Level 20–30 Dark Mongrel

Encountered: Always available in Highlands

CATRIN HAGGARTY

Level 20–40 Ashwinder Duelist

Encountered: Natty Relationship Quest 1: "The Lost Child"

GRODBIK

Level 30–40 Loyalist Sentinel

Encountered: "Rescue Tobbs"

GWENDOLYN ZHOU

Level 30–40 Ashwinder Duelist

Encountered: Natty Relationship Quest 2: "A Basis for Blackmail"

QUAGMIRE TROLL

Level 30–40 Forest Troll

Encountered: Always available in Highlands

DUNSTAN TRINITY

Level 35–40 Ashwinder Executioner

Encountered: "Rescuing Rococo" and "The Hippogriff Marks the Spot"

SILVANUS SELWYN

Level 40 Ashwinder Executioner

Encountered: "Sacking Selwyn"

IONA MORGAN

Level 30 Poacher Duelist

Encountered: "The Hippogriff Marks the Spot"

THE ABSCONDER

Level 30–40 Acromantula

Encountered: "Absconder Encounter"

AILSA TRAVERS

Level 33–40 Ashwinder Assassin

Encountered: Treasure Vault 3

LORD OF THE MANOR

Level 33–40 Inferius

Encountered: Treasure Vault 3

For the Record

Secure every trophy and achievement to mark your historic journey. Explore every corner of Hogwarts, the hamlets, dungeons, and wilds in the Highlands beyond. Accept all challenges, vanquish all enemies, master essential spells and the art of potion brewing. Befriend magical beasts. And keep track of all of it here.

☐ **THE SORT WHO MAKES AN ENTRANCE**
Complete the introduction and finish the Sorting Ceremony
Unlocked upon being sorted into any of the four houses by the Sorting Hat during the introduction.

☐ **THE TOAST OF THE TOWN**
Find the Map Chamber as a Slytherin
Unlocked after speaking with Percival in the Map Chamber during "Jackdaw's Rest" while playing as a Slytherin.

☐ **THE AUROR'S APPRENTICE**
Find the Map Chamber as a Hufflepuff
Unlocked after speaking with Percival in the Map Chamber during "Jackdaw's Rest" while playing as a Hufflepuff.

☐ **THE GRYFFINDOR IN THE GRAVEYARD**
Find the Map Chamber as a Gryffindor
Unlocked after speaking with Percival in the Map Chamber during "Jackdaw's Rest" while playing as a Gryffindor.

☐ **THE WISE OWL**
Find the Map Chamber as a Ravenclaw
Unlocked after speaking with Percival in the Map Chamber during "Jackdaw's Rest" while playing as a Ravenclaw.

☐ **FIRST CLASS STUDENT**
Attend your first class
Unlocked upon completing any of the first two available class missions: "Charms Class" or "Defense Against the Dark Arts (DADA)."

☐ **TROLL WITH THE PUNCHES**
Survive the troll attack on Hogsmeade
Unlocked upon defeating all enemies during the attack on Hogsmeade, accompanied by Natsai or Sebastian.

☐ **THAT'S A KEEPER**
Meet Charles Rookwood in the Map Chamber
Unlocked upon meeting Charles Rookwood in the Map Chamber, ahead of the second trial.

☐ **RISING FROM THE ASHES**
Rescue the phoenix
Rescue the phoenix on behalf of Deek.

GRAPPLING WITH A GRAPHORN
Subdue the Lord of the Shore
Unlocked after completing the "Final Pensieve" quest.

THE ONE WHO MASTERED MEMORIES
View all Pensieves' memories
Unlocked after revelations in the final Pensieve Chamber.

THE HALLOWED HERO
Wield a Deathly Hallow
Unlocked upon completing "The Polyjuice Plot" quest.

THE HERO OF HOGWARTS
Defeat Ranrok
Unlocked upon completing "The Final Repository" quest.

THE SEEKER OF KNOWLEDGE
Win the House Cup
Complete all end-of-year activities, which include winning the House Cup.

THE AVENGING GAZELLE
Complete Natsai Onai's relationship line
Unlocked after your last conversation with Natty in her relationship storyline.

THE DEFENDER OF DRAGONS
Save a dragon
Save the dragon during the "Fire and Vice" quest.

BEAST FRIENDS
Complete Poppy Sweeting's relationship line
Unlocked after your last conversation with Poppy in her relationship storyline.

A SALLOW GRAVE
Complete Sebastian Sallow's relationship line
Unlocked after your last conversation with Sebastian in his relationship storyline.

FLIGHT THE GOOD FLIGHT
Beat Imelda's time in all broom races
Finish first in all broom races during the "Flight Test" quest.

THE GOOD SAMARITAN
Complete all Side Quests
Unlocked upon completing all fifty-nine Side Quests.

CHALLENGE ACCEPTED
Complete all tiers of a challenge
Complete the last level of any challenge for the first time.

COLLECTOR'S EDITION
Complete all collections
Get a check mark for all your collections in the Field Guide.

A KEEN SENSE OF SPELL
Invoke ancient magic for the first time
Land your ancient magic finisher on an enemy for the first time.

LOOM FOR IMPROVEMENT
Upgrade a piece of gear
Upgrade a piece of gear for the first time during "Interior Decorating."

THE ROOT OF THE PROBLEM
Stun ten different enemies using a Mandrake
Unlocked upon stunning ten different enemies using Mandrakes.

THE NATURE OF THE BEAST
Breed every type of beast (except phoenix)
Breed each of the following beasts:
- [ ] Jobberknoll
- [ ] Puffskein
- [ ] Niffler
- [ ] Mooncalf
- [ ] Diricawl
- [ ] Fwooper
- [ ] Thestral
- [ ] Giant Purple Toad
- [ ] Hippogriff
- [ ] Kneazle
- [ ] Unicorn
- [ ] Graphorn

GOING THROUGH THE POTIONS
Brew every type of potion
Unlocked upon having brewed all of the following required potions:
- [ ] Wiggenweld Potion
- [ ] Edurus Potion
- [ ] Maxima Potion
- [ ] Invisibility Potion
- [ ] Focus Potion
- [ ] Thunderbrew

Sleeping Toadstools

PUT DOWN ROOTS
Grow every type of plant
Plant the seeds and grow to
maturity all of the following
required plants:
- Chinese Chomping Cabbage
- Dittany
- Fluxweed
- Knotgrass
- Mandrake
- Mallowsweet
- Shrivelfig
- Venomous Tentacula

THIRD TIME'S A CHARM
**Upgrade a piece of gear
three times**
Unlocked upon upgrading any
piece of Rare, Epic, or Legendary
gear to Level 3.

A TALENT FOR SPENDING
Spend five talent points
Unlocked upon spending a total
of five talent points.

SAVVY SPENDER
Spend all talent points
Unlocked upon spending all of
your talent points.

ROOM WITH A VIEW
Reach the highest point in the
castle: the headmaster's upper
study.

SPILLED MILK
Use *Flipendo* ten times, to tip one
cow or several standing together.

FLOO AROUND THE WORLD
Unlock all Floo Flames
Find and activate all Fast Travel
locations.

FOLLOWED THE BUTTERFLIES
Follow butterflies to a treasure
Complete one "Follow the
Butterflies" event, anywhere
in the world.

RISE TO THE CHALLENGES
**Defeat enemies in all battle
arenas**
Earned after conquering all battle
arenas.

MERLIN'S BEARD!
Complete all Merlin Trials.

THE INTREPID EXPLORER
Discover all cairn dungeons
Unlocked upon discovering all
cairn dungeon entrances.

COASTING ALONG
Visit Poidsear Coast
Unlocked upon arriving anywhere
in the Poidsear Coast region for the
first time.

DEMIGUISE DREAD
Find all Demiguise statues
Find and collect the Cadmean
Moon from all Demiguise statues for
the caretaker.

Mallowsweet

THE ENDS PETRIFY THE MEANS

Defeat a total of fifty enemies using *Petrificus Totalus*.

RAISING EXPECTATIONS

Reach a combo of 100

Land hits without breaking your combo until you pass 100.

FINISHING TOUCHES

Use ancient magic on every enemy in the game:

- Mountain Troll
- Forest Troll
- River Troll
- Stoneback Dugbog
- Great Spined Dugbog
- Cottongrass Dugbog
- Inferius
- Dark Mongrel
- Mongrel
- Poacher Tracker
- Poacher Ranger
- Poacher Stalker
- Poacher Animagus
- Poacher Duelist
- Poacher Executioner
- Ashwinder Scout
- Ashwinder Ranger
- Ashwinder Soldier
- Ashwinder Assassin
- Ashwinder Duelist
- Ashwinder Executioner
- Thornback Scurriour
- Thornback Shooter
- Thornback Ambusher
- Thornback Matriarch
- Venomous Scurriour
- Venomous Shooter
- Venomous Ambusher
- Venomous Matriarch
- Loyalist Warrior
- Loyalist Ranger
- Loyalist Sentinel
- Loyalist Commander
- Loyalist Assassin

THE SPELL MASTER

Learn all spells

Unlock all spells, except Unforgivable Curses:

- *Accio*
- *Alohomora*
- Alteration (Transformation)
- Ancient Magic Throw
- *Arresto Momentum*
- *Bombarda*
- *Confringo*
- Conjuration
- *Depulso*
- *Descendo*
- *Diffindo*
- Disillusionment
- *Evanesco*
- *Expelliarmus*
- *Flipendo*
- *Glacius*
- *Incendio*
- *Levioso*
- *Lumos*
- *Petrificus Totalus*
- *Protego*
- *Reparo*
- *Revelio*
- *Stupefy*
- Transformation (Transformation Highlands)
- *Wingardium Leviosa*

A FORTE FOR ACHIEVEMENT

Reach Level 40

Unlock upon reaching Level 40.

Enemy Types

Being prepared is a combat basic: "forewarned is forearmed," as the saying goes. Here is an overview of the various enemy groups you'll face, with notes obtained from the battlefield.

DARK WIZARDS

Ashwinder Scout
Low-ranking and inexperienced, but strong in number.

Ashwinder Ranger
Strike from a distance while you are engaged in the fray.

Ashwinder Soldier
Fierce and proficient, they will confidently trade blows.

Ashwinder Assassin
Their powerful magic leaves you vulnerable to other attacks.

Ashwinder Duelist
The most brutal and expert fighters among Rookwood's lot.

Ashwinder Executioner
All their attacks hit hard, and they have tanklike stamina.

Poacher Tracker
Not much more than grunts, but don't discount the damage.

Poacher Ranger
Be sure to scan the high ground for these skillful snipers.

Poacher Stalker
As the name suggests, they will pursue you to end the fight.

Poacher Animagus
Be wary of these wizards who can transfigure to become wolves.

Poacher Duelist
The captains of their faction, demonstrating tactical know-how.

Poacher Executioner
They soak up damage while dealing heavy attacks, making them hard to avoid.

DEATHLY ENEMIES

Death's Shadow
Hunters that are alert to the slightest movement or sound.

Death's Troll
Attack in number and at speed, forcing you out from hiding places.

Death's Dark Mongrel
Swift and relentless in pursuit, covering distance shockingly fast.

DRAGONS

Green Welsh
A green dragon native to Wales. It will only attack humans if provoked.

Hebridean Black
A large aggressive dragon. It is named for the Hebridean islands of Scotland.

Hungarian Horntail
The fiercest and most dangerous dragon breed.

DUGBOGS

Stoneback Dugbog
A Dugbog that inhabits coastal areas. Slow on land but dangerous in the water.
Drops Dugbog Tongue

Great Spined Dugbog
A Dugbog that inhabits lake areas. Slow on land but dangerous in the water.
Drops Dugbog Tongue

Cottongrass Dugbog
A Dugbog that inhabits marsh areas. Slow on land but dangerous in the water.
Drops Dugbog Tongue

GOBLINS

Loyalist Warrior
They may be small, but be wary of their intellect and magic power.

Loyalist Ranger
Sneaky, and terribly accurate with their highly damaging crossbows.

Loyalist Sentinel
Seek to incapacitate their prey with spells, leaving you vulnerable.

Loyalist Commander
Heavily armed and aggressive. Defeat them first to spook their minions.

Loyalist Assassin
They vanish before appearing right beside you to deliver crushing blows.

SPIDERS

Venomous Hatchling
Minuscule and extremely agile, their low damage is still a concern.

Venomous Scurriour
Spits venom at its prey, causing considerable damage over time.
Drops Spider Fang

Venomous Shooter
Shoots webs to entangle—you are immobilized until you can break free.
Drops Spider Fang

Venomous Ambusher
Beware their bite, and their movement, which is hard to track.
Drops Spider Fang

Venomous Matriarch
A horribly large, highly aggressive, and deadly venomous spider.
Drops Spider Fang

Thornback Hatchling
Newly hatched spiders from egg sacs that can be blasted as they scurry.

Thornback Scurriour
Crawls upon every surface possible to rapidly gain ground.
Drops Spider Fang

Thornback Shooter
These spit at you from afar, so be aware of their changing positions.
Drops Spider Fang

Thornback Ambusher
They tunnel toward your position. Strike them as they emerge.
Drops Spider Fang

Thornback Matriarch
Angrily, and most effectively, defends her nest from visitors.
Drops Spider Fang

Acromantula
Believed to have been bred by wizards to guard residences and treasures.
Drops Spider Fang

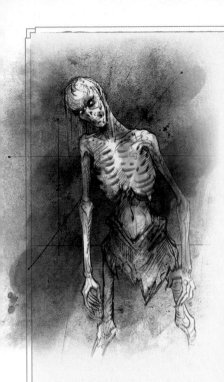

INFERI

Inferius
A reanimated corpse now under the control of a Dark wizard.
Drops Stench of the Dead

SOLDIERS

Guardian
Single-minded in their efforts to stop intruders.

Pensieve Guardian
Colossal foe in Percival Rackam's Trial, with stomps that send shock waves.

Pensieve Sentry
Melee specialists, marching incessantly toward you in order to smite you.

Pensieve Sentinel
Known to leap high into the rafters so that they might land on top of you.

Pensieve Protector
Soldiers created by the Keepers to aid in the protection of ancient magic.

TROLLS

Forest Troll
A ferocious troll that dwells in the Dark Forest and doesn't give up easily.
Drops Troll Mucus

Mountain Troll
A sturdy troll that lives in rocky and high-altitude climates and favors charging.
Drops Troll Mucus

River Troll
A species of troll that makes its nest near rivers and bodies of water.
Drops Troll Mucus

Armored Troll
Dominates tight spaces, and best tackled with a partner to distract.
Drops Troll Mucus

WOLF

Mongrel
Flighty, and likely to be one leap ahead of wherever you take aim.
Drops Mongrel Fur

Dark Mongrel
Vicious wolves that stalk the wilds surrounding Hogwarts in packs.
Drops Mongrel Fur

Magical Beasts

Soon after Beasts Class with Professor Howin, your house-elf friend Deek presents you with the nab-sack. You can use this to rescue magical beasts and rear them in vivariums in your Room of Requirement.

Keeping beasts brushed, fed, and amused makes them happy, and contented beasts shed by-products such as feathers and fur. These bestow magical properties upon clothing that is woven using your Enchanted Loom.

Additional by-products can be purchased from Brood & Peck in Hogsmeade, and Indira Wolff in the hamlet of Bàgh an Taigh. Specialist by-products for the Jobberknoll, Mooncalf, Niffler, and Puffskein are only sold by Bernard Ndiaye in Irondale.

As your expertise grows, and your beasts flourish, Deek teaches you how to breed beasts to deliver offspring. You may then use a breeding pen for your beasts, all except the phoenix.

FWOOPER
Toy: Quaffle Ball (acquired from a chest in the Swamp Vivarium)
By-product: Fwooper Feather
Regions:
Hogwarts Valley
Feldcroft

DIRICAWL
Toy: Tumbleweed (acquired from a chest in the Swamp Vivarium)
By-product: Diricawl Feather
Regions:
Poidsear Coast
Marunweem Lake
Clagmar Coast
Hogwarts Valley
North Hogwarts

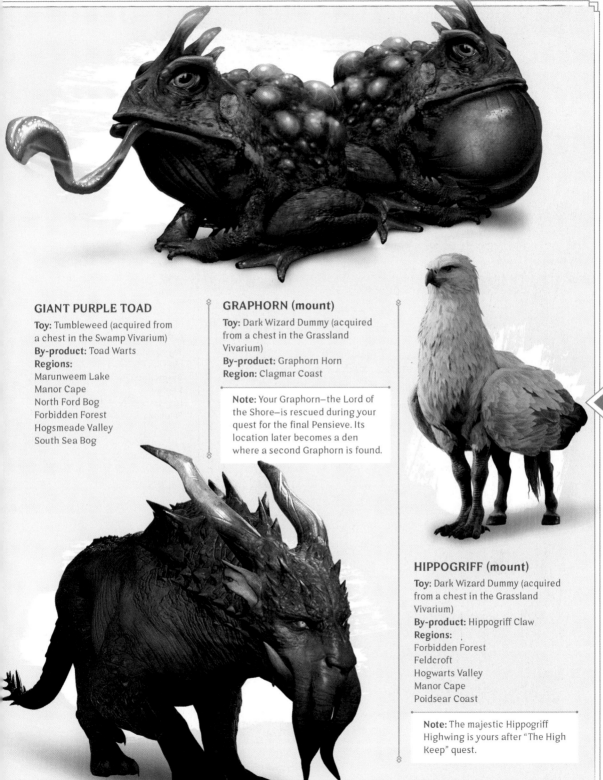

GIANT PURPLE TOAD

Toy: Tumbleweed (acquired from a chest in the Swamp Vivarium)
By-product: Toad Warts
Regions:
Marunweem Lake
Manor Cape
North Ford Bog
Forbidden Forest
Hogsmeade Valley
South Sea Bog

GRAPHORN (mount)

Toy: Dark Wizard Dummy (acquired from a chest in the Grassland Vivarium)
By-product: Graphorn Horn
Region: Clagmar Coast

> **Note:** Your Graphorn—the Lord of the Shore—is rescued during your quest for the final Pensieve. Its location later becomes a den where a second Graphorn is found.

HIPPOGRIFF (mount)

Toy: Dark Wizard Dummy (acquired from a chest in the Grassland Vivarium)
By-product: Hippogriff Claw
Regions:
Forbidden Forest
Feldcroft
Hogwarts Valley
Manor Cape
Poidsear Coast

> **Note:** The majestic Hippogriff Highwing is yours after "The High Keep" quest.

JOBBERKNOLL

Toy: Quaffle Ball (acquired from a chest in the Swamp Vivarium)
By-product: Jobberknoll Feather
Regions:
Marunweem Lake
Cragcroftshire
Manor Cape
Forbidden Forest
South Hogwarts
Feldcroft

Note: The Jobberknoll is one of the first beasts you'll rescue, helped along by Deek.

MOONCALF

Toy: Moon Ball (acquired from a chest in the Swamp Vivarium)
By-product: Mooncalf Fur
Regions:
Feldcroft
South Hogwarts
Forbidden Forest
Poidsear Coast

KNEAZLE

Toy: Yarn Ball (acquired from a chest in the Grassland Vivarium)
By-product: Kneazle Whiskers

Regions:
South Sea Bog
Hogwarts Valley
Hogsmeade Valley
Clagmar Coast
Cragcroftshire
Marunweem Lake

NIFFLER

Toy: Gold Ball (acquired from a chest in the Swamp Vivarium)
By-product: Niffler Fur
Regions:
Cragcroftshire
North Hogwarts
Feldcroft
Hogwarts Valley
South Hogwarts
Hogsmeade Valley
North Ford Bog
Manor Cape
Poidsear Coast

THESTRAL

Toy: Bone Ball (acquired from a chest in the Swamp Vivarium)
By-product: Thestral Hair
Regions:
Marunweem Lake
North Ford Bog

PHOENIX

Toy: Quaffle Ball (acquired from a chest in the Swamp Vivarium)
By-product: Phoenix Feather
Region: Poidsear Coast (Dungeon)

> **Note:** There is only one unique phoenix. Impress Deek to learn of its location.

UNICORN

Toy: Bubble Toy (acquired from a chest in the Grassland Vivarium)
By-product: Unicorn Hair
Region: Forbidden Forest

PUFFSKEIN

Toy: Bogey Ball (acquired from a chest in the Swamp Vivarium)
By-product: Puffskein Fur
Regions:
North Hogwarts
Forbidden Forest
Manor Cape
Feldcroft
Clagmar Coast
Poidsear Coast

> **Note:** The Puffskein is one of the first beasts you'll rescue, under Deek's instruction.

Gaming Notes

ISBN 978-1-338-76765-0

10 9 8 7 6 5 4   23 24 25 26 27

Printed in the U.S.A.   40

First printing 2023

Written by Paul Davies and Kate Lewis

Project Management and Design by Amazing15

Special thanks to Duncan Harris